THE
CHIEF EXECUTIVE OPERATING SYSTEM

THE ESSENTIAL PLAYBOOK
FOR SUCCESS IN THE CEO ROLE

JOEL TRAMMELL
AND
SHERIF SAKR

Published by P180 Press
Austin, Texas

For information on bulk purchases, please email info@AmericanCEO.com.

Design and composition by Sheila Parr
Cover design by Sheila Parr
Cover image used under license from © The Noun Project / Valter Bispo

ISBN 13: 979-8-9851957-2-9

CONTENTS

For all those who are taking the lonely walk across the CEO tightrope.

Note: In the text, "I" refers to Joel and "we" refers to Joel and Sherif.

INTRODUCTION

When I started my professional career in the late 1980s, information about how to run a business was hard to come by.

In high school, I had been fortunate to meet two successful businesspeople. We would now call them *entrepreneurs*, but you didn't hear that word used much in those days. I peppered them with questions about their various businesses and how they worked. Later, when I started my first business, I was still hungry to learn everything I could about running a business. Unfortunately, it was almost impossible to find pertinent information on the subject. My local bookstore and library had a few business-related titles but nothing very practical for an entrepreneur starting their first venture.

Fast-forward to today and the Internet is full of sites that discuss in detail how to start and grow a business. You can choose from tens of thousands of business books on Amazon.com. There are business coaches and trainers galore. (I certainly could have used these resources back in the day. You'd howl with laughter at the amateurism of the presentation my wife and I used in the late 1990s as a startup to raise $11 million.)

This proliferation of resources around entrepreneurship reflects how most trades and specialties develop over time. At first you have innovators who develop their techniques through trial and error, usually relying on their natural talent. New entrants to the field are locked out unless they can jump in and learn on the fly. But as time passes, the field becomes *professionalized*: a body of knowledge, best practices, and tools comes into being. Practitioners develop accepted ways of doing things, and these resources become available as a guide to new entrants.

Another example is the professionalization of sales. When I started my career, the typical business-to-business salesperson was a walking Rolodex. They leveraged their precious contacts to drive sales, and success was all about who you knew and how hard you pounded the pavement. If an employer threatened to fire one of these lone-wolf salespeople, the rep would simply take their Rolodex down the road to a competitor. But over time, the "who you know" approach transformed into a process-driven approach enabled by technology. Success in sales became less about your contact list and individual persuasiveness and much more about having the right knowledge and tools.

I still remember the day in January 2001 when my recently hired director of sales approached me about using a new technology to run his sales group. I asked him to tell me about it. He said it was a network-based technology that would store all our contacts and opportunities in a database at a remote data center (*the cloud* was not in the lexicon at this point). I remember asking, "Where is this remote data center?"

He said he didn't know. Huh.

Then I asked how he was going to get all the salespeople to enter their data in the database; all the salespeople I had known treated their contacts as their most prized and secret possession.

He said he would fire them if they didn't. Huh again.

And then came the clincher. I asked him how much this technology cost. This was a time when the traditional on-site contact management solution for a sales team could easily run into the hundreds of thousands of dollars. He said it would cost just $10 per salesperson per month. I laughed out loud.

I repeated what he'd told me. "So, you're saying you are going to get all your salespeople to enter our most sensitive data into a database stored you don't know where, and it costs only $10 per month?" He said I had it right. Since he had only reported to me for a few weeks, I thought it was important that I explain to him how things worked. I said that normally, when an executive comes to me with an idea and I say go ahead, I take responsibility for the outcome. If it blows up, don't worry, I have your back. But in this case, I wanted to be absolutely clear: If this blows up, it's your fault. If you are okay with that, go ahead. He said he was—and the rest is history.

The product was Salesforce.com, and over the next eight years, we built our business around the product. This gave us a tremendous competitive advantage. It was the best decision I *didn't* make as CEO. Using Salesforce.com and strong management skills, my head of sales built a super successful, highly predictive sales organization that delivered thirty-one consecutive quarters of double-digit year-over-year growth. When we surveyed our customers to find out why they bought from us, they cited "the professionalism of the sales team" as the number-one reason. We had become early adopters of Salesforce.com just as the field of sales was rapidly professionalizing, and it benefitted us tremendously.

Twenty years later, the sales function is solidly professionalized. The lone wolf with his Rolodex is a relic. Good sales teams thrive on strong processes and metrics. And if you interview a sales executive who doesn't talk about their process and a data-driven approach, they are considered incompetent.

Similar transformations have taken place across most functions of business, from HR to marketing to customer service. Each of these areas—along with the very process of starting a business, as we saw before—is now supported by a foundation of tested, learnable concepts and tools. A new entrant can jump in and learn how success is typically achieved. They might later decide to break the mold, but there is a mold to break in the first place, one that is widely used by professionals at the top of their game.

The professionalization process has hit every corner of business except for one: *the role of the chief executive.*

PROFESSIONALIZING THE CEO ROLE

Currently, CEOs take on their job without a well-defined body of knowledge to rely on. There is no clear guidance on what a CEO actually does, and little agreement about how to approach the role. There is no set of effective practices that can be refined for a given situation. Generic leadership books rarely cover the highly specific nuts and bolts of the job.

That leads most CEOs to rely on charisma, daring, and a lot of luck. They have to learn on the job, and in a vacuum. Is it any wonder that most of them fail? The rate is between 50 and 70 percent, depending upon how you count. These are people who have been incredibly successful at every job they had before (if they hadn't, they wouldn't have gotten to be CEO), yet this one role proves the exception. The new CEO is like a sixteen-year-old who gets handed the keys to a Porsche with no training other than "Just drive between the lines!" Only with great luck would such a kid avoid wrecking the car.

We wrote this book to offer a framework for success in the CEO role at scale, and hopefully to move forward the professionalization of the role itself. My first book, *The CEO Tightrope*, aimed to give CEOs a manual to the job based on decades of experience, study, and observation. This book uses the contents of *The CEO Tightrope* as a foundation to create what we call the Chief Executive Operating System (CEO-S)—a first-of-its-kind framework for success in the CEO role.

The Chief Executive Operating System is both shorter and more action-oriented than *The CEO Tightrope*. We're not interested in academic exercises. We want to offer CEOs—new, seasoned, or aspiring—a practical, systematic way to approach this vital position. We want to look past the mystique of the role and give you a pragmatic resource for getting the right things done. Because our primary aim is to present the operating system itself, we will not linger at length on any one topic. Rather, the Chief Executive Operating System is intended as a framework—a structure you can use to organize your future learning and experience. With the operating system in place, you have a robust mental model for understanding the fundamentals of the CEO role. You can then refine the operating system for the remainder of your career, growing your capability each year. (At AmericanCEO.com/reading-list, we have compiled some of our favorite resources you can use to deepen your understanding of the various parts of the system.)

The Chief Executive Operating System applies to businesses of any size but primarily addresses the "pure" or "real" CEO role that becomes necessary at around the one-hundred-employee mark. This is not to imply that CEOs of smaller organizations are not legitimate CEOs; rather it is to acknowledge that the job transforms in nature around that point. We want to prepare you for that moment if you're not there and offer guidance if you are. Also, when we mention "business" throughout this book, we refer to both for-profit and nonprofit organizations.

The Chief Executive Operating System is divided into three sections: People, Execution, and You.

The first section, **PEOPLE**, explores how to effectively work with people at all levels of the organization from the CEO seat. One thing we love about the CEO role is that the only way for a CEO to be successful is by working through other people and helping *them* be successful. The concepts in this section emphasize the reality that CEOs haven't risen to a level where they can leave the "people stuff" to others. In fact, the "people stuff" is now more critical than ever.

The second section, **EXECUTION**, is about converting strategy into operational excellence through the five responsibilities of a CEO. These five responsibilities, first described in *The CEO Tightrope*, are the CEO's bread and butter. Done well, they lead to a highly functional organization that delivers predictable performance.

The third section, **YOU**, discusses how CEOs can prioritize their own continuous development and become more mindful. The CEO role is arguably the most demanding in business, and it requires not only constant self-education but also a healthy perspective and a sense of work-life balance.

Unsurprisingly, there is much overlap between these sections. An exercise in one area may have a positive impact in another area entirely. For example, you may be thinking you're making a decision about resources, but you find it also impacts the culture and how you hire. This is the nature of the Chief Executive Operating System, which was designed as a holistic system. All the concepts are intertwined into a self-contained whole.

Ultimately, **applying the Chief Executive Operating System will allow you to deliver on your most fundamental job: to deliver predictable performance on behalf of the organization**. A lot of good stuff comes along with that, from higher valuations and ability to exit to great career prospects for you. But this doesn't mean that the CEO's job is just about monetary and career success. As CEO, you get to elevate from a life of success, focused on you, to a life of *significance*, focused on the success of others. Our hope is that by strengthening your performance as CEO, we also help you grow your ability to have a positive impact on the lives and well-being of every person who works for or with your organization.

CEO SUPPORT SYSTEMS

This book aims to give you an operating system, a way to understand and apply the fundamentals of the CEO role. But certainly no book can, on its own, make you a great CEO. It will take consistent use of these principles, deeper learning about each area of the system, and—hopefully—support from people who want to see you become the best leader you can be.

The CEO role is notoriously lonely, with the CEO often feeling they have no one to turn to or unburden themselves on. This leads many CEOs to seek help from support figures like executive coaches. We are enthusiastic proponents of this. It is useful, however, to understand the different types of support available to the CEO and what they do, and do not, offer.

A **CEO coach** is an accountability system and sounding board for the chief executive. You tell them what you want to work on, and they'll help you do it. As a neutral observer, they reflect back what they see and hear from you in an effort to help you grow as a leader. But they don't come to an engagement with answers to your business dilemmas—they help you come to the answer on your own. Typically, the coach doesn't supply information or content of their own. They are a little like a therapist or a mentor in that they start by understanding your background, your current situation, and your aspirations, then work from there.

A **consultant**, on the other hand, does give you answers. They come in and assess your business model, the market, internal processes, and more, then make concrete suggestions for improvement. These might not be the right answers, but they'll give them to you. They are usually less focused on how you are doing in the CEO role and more focused on the business overall.

Peer groups are another support system for CEOs. These can be an invaluable source of reinforcement and guidance for the CEO. The simple fact of sitting with people who understand what you are dealing with as head of the organization is huge for a lot of people. It's also a great way to glean insights from leaders in other industries, learn from the successes and failures of people who have been there, and seek input on specific dilemmas you may be facing.

A **CEO trainer** is the rarest breed. It's what we personally have a passion for doing; this book is part of that mission, as are the CEO trainings we offer through our company, American CEO. The CEO trainer offers a framework for doing the job of the CEO, as we do with the Chief Executive Operating System described in this book. They show you specific strategies and tools, how to do the things your organization needs and requires from its CEO. Where the CEO coach is the cheerleader and accountability partner, the CEO trainer is the educator and guide.

To get the most out of the support systems you choose, be sure you understand your own goals and what you want out of the engagement, then opt for the partner or partners that make the most sense.

PART I
PEOPLE

IT BEGINS AND
ENDS WITH PEOPLE

No one gets to the role of CEO without knowing how to work with people. Yet first-time CEOs quickly find that the job comes packaged with a whole new set of human-related challenges—things they aren't necessarily used to dealing with.

One of these challenges is the CEO's obligation to be equally responsible for all departments of the organization. These departments may be full of people who are temperamentally very different from the CEO, doing work the CEO doesn't quite understand. It is important to understand the needs and interests of these disparate groups and then balance them against those of other departments. Other people-related challenges of the CEO role are simply intensifications of dynamics that exist for any manager: How do you gain employees' trust, understand their motivations, and lead them effectively?

Ultimately, the CEO's success depends on their ability to

master these and other people-related challenges. That's why the Chief Executive Operating System is a people-centric approach to business, and why we begin with effective people management. Starting with people rather than with metrics (though we'll get to that later) is something CEOs have repeatedly expressed appreciation for as they learn the Chief Executive Operating System.

Here are three reasons why CEOs should see their job as first and foremost about people.

1. *The CEO's contribution is made through others, not through individual work.* Around the time a company passes the hundred-employee milestone, the chief executive's job becomes what we call a "real" or "pure" CEO role. This means the CEO has to give up doing the individual work and influence others to get the right things done.

   Most of us started our careers by being good at delivering some particular type of work. If, like us, you have an engineering degree, maybe you started out building great products. If you came up in sales, maybe you were great at closing big deals. If you cut your teeth in accounting, maybe you were great at building sophisticated financial models. In each case, you were judged on an outcome that you delivered largely on your own. This is sharply different from leadership roles, particularly the CEO role. Though you're on the hook for the company's output, you've got to get it done *through other people.* **Your fundamental unit of operation before was tasks. Now, it is people.** As CEO, you can't possibly manage or even know about all the tasks necessary to deliver exceptional performance. You must take a higher-level approach, showing people the desired destination and empowering them to help you get there.

2. *Every mature business is in the people business.* The people-centric approach is important because once the business has reached a certain size, its success is no longer about a specific product or industry; success is now all about people. In the early days of a business, the mission is to figure out how to sell a product or service without running out of cash—i.e., how to achieve product-market fit. Once that's done, the nature of growth changes. Now, you can no longer grow by just selling more, because each new sale puts additional demand on the organization. Functions like marketing, human resources, legal, and finance are increasingly required. At this point, **the only way to sustainably grow the business is to master the ability to hire well and ensure there are productive and talented people across all business functions.** Treating people well—by empowering them, supporting them, and helping them achieve their goals—is not only the right thing to do. It is also the most successful way to run a business.

3. *People (really) are your most important asset.* In many businesses today, people-related expenses make up 70 percent or more of the budget. Leaders frequently say that "people are our company's most important asset," but a good CEO does more than lip service. They know that if they are spending most of the budget on people, they should devote a similar proportion of their time and effort to optimizing that precious resource.

    The good news for you is that most of your competitors are not spending an appropriate amount of time focused on their people. This presents an opportunity to create a significant competitive advantage. If you focus closely on your people capacity as CEO—including how you attract, hire, engage, and retain talent—you will put yourself well ahead of the pack.

Let's now look at a core people-related concept of the Chief Executive Operating System: how the CEO can manage tensions between the six key groups that comprise the business.

TRIANGLES
OF TENSION

At its core, the CEO's job is a balancing act between the interests of several distinct groups.

A useful model for thinking about this fact can be found in the definition of a business. Here's the working definition we use:

> A business is a group of people who provide a product or service to a market for the benefit of customers, employees, and shareholders.[1]

---

1 More broadly, "shareholders" refers to the controlling interests of a business. For a corporation, the controlling interest is shareholders. In other cases, the controlling interest might be a single owner or, in the case of a nonprofit, a board of trustees.

If we pick apart this definition, we can identify three core functional groups within the business and three core constituencies the business serves. The three core functional groups are contained in the first part of the definition:

A business is a group of people who **provide** a **product or service** to a **market** . . .

These three internal groups are the Product or Service group (those who create the offerings of the company), the Marketing group (those who position the product or service within a market), and the Sales group (those who facilitate the exchange of value between the company and the market). They form the first Triangle of Tension the CEO must understand:

You are likely familiar with some of the tensions that arise from these three groups, as each one values fundamentally different things. Sales values closing deals. Marketing values maximizing the brand. And the Product/Service group values the quality of whatever is being delivered. As CEO, you sit outside these groups and are responsible for ensuring that all of these interests are properly represented, with no groups running roughshod over the others. Sales shouldn't make promises on which the Product/Service group can't deliver. The Product/Service group can't make something they think is cool but that the market won't buy. And so on.

The second Triangle of Tension is contained in the back half of our definition of a business:

. . . for the benefit of **customers**, **employees**, and **shareholders**.

These are the core constituencies the business serves, and again they have interrelated but competing interests. Customers would like a high-quality product at the lowest price possible. Employees would like as much pay as possible. And shareholders, or the controlling interest, want maximum efficiency and the biggest return they can get. To be successful over the long term, a CEO must balance the needs of these groups to build a sustainable enterprise.

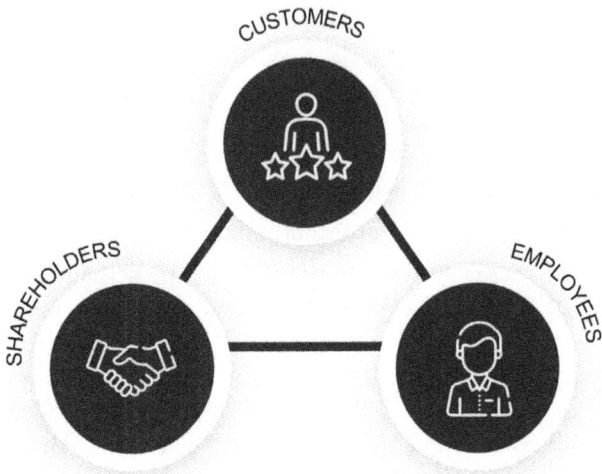

Taken together, the Triangles of Tension form a model for how the CEO should think about their entire company and the various groups of people involved.

The Triangles can also be viewed as a framework for a basic organizational chart, with one executive role representing each of the functions and constituencies. After an organization reaches a certain size, it will likely have an executive heading up Sales, Marketing, and Product/Service, as well as an executive representing shareholders (the CFO), the employees (a CHRO, Head of People, etc.), and customers (a customer service executive).

The customer service executive is the least common, often placed under a sales or product executive. We regard that as a fundamental mistake that creates an imbalance among the core constituencies. It is imperative that the person representing the voice of the customer have their own seat at the executive table, just like those representing the other five groups.

At the end of this chapter, we will encourage you to create your own org chart, showing who represents each point on the Triangles of Tension, and then share the org chart with your team. If your company is small, you may not have an executive team built out. It's not unusual to see a company of twenty employees with a CEO who performs all or most of these functions. If that's you, write your own name in the boxes for the functions you run. This shows the organization (and reminds you) that these roles will need to be handed off as the business grows. Beyond the startup stage, it's vital that each group is represented by someone who specializes in the fundamentals of that area. Once the organization exceeds one hundred employees, those leaders should be in place, each empowered to build up their own group. This frees up the CEO to focus exclusively on the CEO role—facilitating between the six groups, working in the white space inside and between the triangles.

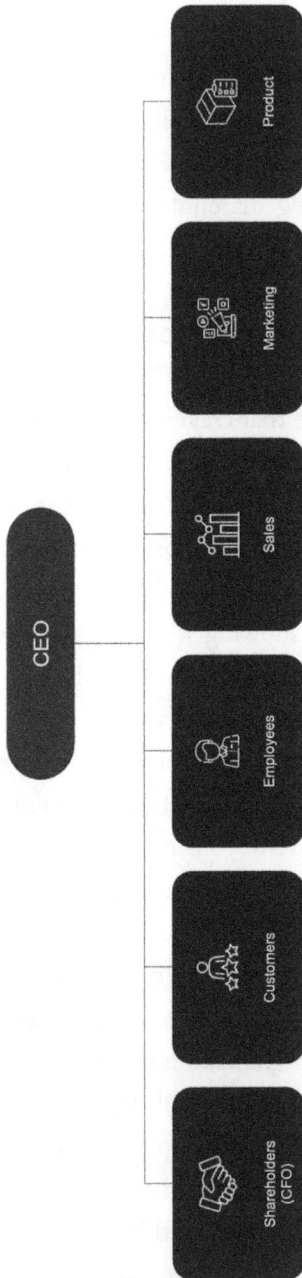

RELATIONAL COMPLEXITY IN THE GROWING ORGANIZATION

What is it about this hundred-person threshold that requires the CEO to move into the "pure" chief executive role? It's not a magic number, and for some organization, the benchmark may be at fifty or seventy-five employees. But simple human nature requires that, somewhere around this size, the CEO's role transforms from directly helping within the triangles to stepping back and viewing them as an interrelated whole.

This is largely because there are simply too many human relationships within the organization for one person to manage. At twenty people, the CEO can have a personal relationship with every employee, and every employee can have a personal relationship with each other. With twenty people, there are only 190 total relationships possible in the whole organization. And it's relatively easy for the CEO to keep twenty people aligned when they all have some knowledge of what everyone else does and are in regular contact with their colleagues.

However, when the organization grows to one hundred people, the situation is radically different. Going from twenty people to one hundred people isn't five times more complicated as it might first seem—it is actually orders of magnitude more complicated. With one hundred people on the team, there are now 4,950 total relationships possible. That's over twenty-five times as many relationships required for everyone to know what everyone else is doing. By the time the organization grows to five hundred people, there are almost 125,000 total possible relationships! Humans just aren't set up to handle that kind of interaction at scale, which is why the hundred-plus company requires a fundamentally different method of coordination.

This isn't to imply that it's easy being CEO of a twenty-person company. The hardest job either of us has ever done was being CEO of a small, under-resourced organization. However, the job was difficult because at twenty employees, we were also doing four or five of the six fundamental executive roles. At this stage, it is more about keeping your own sanity than keeping everyone on the same page. But to effectively impact an organization at one hundred employees and beyond requires the CEO to take on a job that is dramatically different than the one they had at twenty employees. At its core is understanding and managing the two Triangles of Tension that make up any business.

With that foundation of the Chief Executive Operating System laid, we can now move on to understanding the nature of the individual people who make up these six parts of the organization, including yourself.

TRIANGLES OF TENSION: BUILD YOUR PLAYBOOK

- **Using the two Triangles of Tension as a starting place, draw your organizational structure.** If any of the six areas of the business do not have an executive leader in place, put your name as the leader of that area. Until you hire someone to own that part of the business, you are responsible for leading it. It's a good idea to extend this organizational chart to show where all employees in the organization are located. Today, many software solutions allow you to create an org chart and share it with everyone on the team.

BECOMING FLUENT IN THE LANGUAGE OF PEOPLE

We just established that the CEO's fundamental unit of operation is not tasks or deliverables but *people*. Unless the CEO enables the organization to bring on and fully engage the right people, no mission or vision will ever be achieved. We've also established that the CEO is responsible for balancing the complex interests of various groups of humans within the organization, mediating as tensions arise.

Given that the CEO is first and foremost in the people business, we believe they should have a rich language to describe those people, just as experts in any other field have a specialized vocabulary. If your most important assets are people, and you're going to be judged on how well those people perform, it's not just worthwhile to develop a language for thinking about and talking about them—it's required. In the real world, few CEOs develop this dialect. For a long time, I didn't either.

By the time I graduated from college with an electrical engineering degree, I could describe an electrical circuit in intricate detail. I knew all the definitions of words like *current*, *resistance*, and *voltage* and understood the various mathematical relationships involved in engineering. One might say I was fluent in electrical circuits.

But when it came to people, I was not. If you had asked me to describe my best friend, a guy I had hung out with all through college, I would have been at a loss for words. I might have said he was "smart" and he was "a people person." Did I not know my best friend? Of course I did. I knew him very well. And if you had given me a specific set of circumstances, I could have told you how he would react. What I didn't have was a vocabulary to describe him.

You can try this exercise yourself. Take out a blank sheet of paper and start describing your significant other or best friend. Do it so that someone who had never met them would read your description and understand their personality. Most of us quickly run out of words. That's because most of us don't have a language for thinking about and talking about people.

When it comes to managing, leading, and coaching people, understanding the unique characteristics that each person brings to the table is crucial. Because your success will be determined by the people in your organization, you—along with your executive team and, ideally, anyone in a management role in the company—must become fluent in the language of people.

Fortunately, we don't have to develop a language about people from scratch. During World War I, the US Army began developing personality tests to predict which soldiers would suffer from shellshock. Since then, the personality-testing industry has grown into a multibillion-dollar category with hundreds of players. Today, these tests are widely used in corporate America. Some of their uses are controversial, for good reason. For example, we don't recommend using personality assessments in the hiring process, or to predict the job performance of any individual. There's no good evidence to suggest that this kind of prescriptive application has business value. But there is enormous value in using these tools to develop a common language in the organization for talking about people.

For one thing, understanding the unique nature of an individual helps any leader work with that person more effectively. Once you can process and describe how that person operates, you have the tools necessary for giving them effective feedback, assigning them the right kind of work, gathering information from them, and much, much more. It's also true that a lot of the strife a CEO deals with on a typical day boils down to unacknowledged clashes between people's personalities and working styles. Without a language to process what's really going on, these clashes can feel intractable, constant, and frustrating. But with that language, you can reveal what's going on beneath the surface. For example, it might seem like David and Jennifer are always going to be at each other's throats—until you realize that their disagreements actually reflect two conflicting orientations to the planning process. That's a specific discussion you can have with them.

Your language around people is also vital in balancing the Triangles of Tension. What do you know about the personality of your head of sales, and how can you use that information to help them interact productively with the marketing and product groups? How does your personality mesh with your head of

HR, and what can you do to base that relationship in common understanding? This is the type of work people-fluent CEOs do continuously with every stakeholder they come into contact with.

Finally, developing your fluency in the language of people grows your own self-awareness. We will discuss this topic more fully in Part III. Management guru Peter Drucker once said, "To succeed in this new world, we will have to learn, first, who we are. Few people, even highly successful people, can answer the questions: Do you know what you're good at? Do you know what you need to learn so that you get the full benefit of your strengths? Few have even asked themselves these questions." The assessments we discuss in this chapter are a great way to better understand the unique value you bring to the organization as a leader and the value everyone else brings also.

When we teach the Chief Executive Operating System in person, we start with two key personality assessments: Clifton-Strengths and DISC. These are the tools we have found to be most effective for creating a shared language about people in organizations. They are particularly useful in business because they are simple. But these are certainly not the only tests that work. It's less important which exact tools you use than that you choose one that works for your team. The Myers-Briggs Type Indicator is another popular choice, as are Enneagram, Birkman, and others. Some tools, such as Truity, offer access to multiple assessments at once.

CLIFTONSTRENGTHS

If you have not used personality assessments in your organization before, we suggest starting with CliftonStrengths from Gallup (available for purchase at Gallup.com/CliftonStrengths). We recommend this product because it takes a positive psychology approach, identifying a person's top five strengths from a pool of thirty-four. Peter Drucker said, "A person can perform only from strength. One cannot build performance on weakness, let alone on something one cannot do at all." This focus on strengths is a great starting place for the CEO who wants to build an organization where people can use their natural abilities as much as possible. We encourage you to choose the full assessment that gives you your ranking of the full thirty-four strengths. As you become aware of people's strengths and how they show up in the workplace, you will become comfortable with the vocabulary of the thirty-four strengths. You will begin to think about and discuss people in a productive and positive way.

For example, one of the thirty-four strengths is Activator. People with Activator among their top strengths like to quickly turn thoughts into action. Their motto might be "No time like the present to get started." When leveraged properly, a person with the Activator theme can be a valuable member of a team. As their manager, you will enjoy their willingness to just jump in and get moving. Of course, there can be situations where this leap-before-you-look attitude can cause issues. Enter the Strategic strength. People with Strategic among their top strengths like to examine all possible options before they act. Their motto might be, "What if?" They are look-before-you-leap people, maybe even study-extensively-before-you-leap people. Again, this can be a very valuable skill to have on a team. The challenge is that Activators and Strategics are on opposite ends of a behavioral spectrum and, if asked to work together, may butt up against each other.

I once had a strong Activator type who worked for me in a

marketing role. As an individual contributor, she was a superstar, constantly starting and completing new projects. As the company grew, we needed to expand the group and tapped her to be the manager. A couple of existing employees were assigned to her group. After a few months, this new manager came into my office and began complaining about her employees. She was very frustrated that every time she proposed a new idea, the two employees seemed to push back instead of jumping in. In fact, she was thinking it was about time to fire them. However, I knew that both employees had been rated by their previous manager as superstar performers who consistently produced high-quality work. Why was the new manager not seeing this?

I quickly consulted the employee list to look at the strengths of her two employees. Both employees' top strength was Strategic. What the manager saw as pushback was just their Strategic orientation in play, as they tried to process the new idea and understand where it fit with all the other new ideas the manager had proposed. While an Activator might be comfortable starting a new project every day, a Strategic will need time to process each new project idea to ensure success. As I explained this to the new manager, she quickly grasped what she needed to do. She couldn't ask these Strategic employees to be her sounding board for every new idea that came into her head. Instead, she needed to clearly prioritize which projects were important and allow the Strategics to deliver top-quality results.

Because behavior exists across many different spectrums, there will always be conflict between people who are on opposite ends of the various spectrums. The Activator will view the Strategic as always pushing back and being indecisive. The Strategic will view the Activator as being overly reckless and ill prepared.

As the manager of a team that includes both types, your job is to understand the strengths of everyone on your team and deploy each appropriately to maximize the performance of the entire organization. You will also need to educate your team on the differences between themselves and their coworkers so everyone can facilitate effective collaboration.

As CEO, it is particularly important to understand not only individual strengths, but also the collective strengths and weaknesses of your executive team. Gallup arranges the strengths into four domains: **Executing, Influencing, Relationship Building**, and **Strategic Thinking**. When you map your team's top five strengths into these domains, you may find that you are overall weak in one area or overloaded in another. If, for example, your executives' strengths are clustered in the Strategic Thinking domain, that's something the CEO should be aware of. This type of team could spend a great deal of time planning and theorizing without ensuring the necessary follow-up. Understanding this tendency, the CEO can push discussions toward execution and set up mechanisms that encourage action.

DISC

The other personality assessment we use extensively with our CEO clients is the DISC model, first described by psychologist William Moulton Marston in 1928. Like many innovations, the theory was originally proposed to predict job performance but demonstrated no capacity to do so. What it has proven helpful for is, like CliftonStrengths, describing different behavioral tendencies that can cause stress in the work environment.

The DISC model identifies the following four major

personality profiles: **(D)ominance, (I)nfluence, (S)teadiness, and (C)onscientiousness**. Each type can be characterized as follows:

- **(D)ominance** personalities tend to act assertively and place emphasis on accomplishing numeric results.

- **(I)nfluence** personalities tend to use charm to influence others and place emphasis on enthusiasm and fun.

- **(S)teadiness** personalities tend to be accepting and place emphasis on cooperation and consensus.

- **(C)onscientiousness** personalities tend to focus on details and place emphasis on accuracy, integrity, and competency.

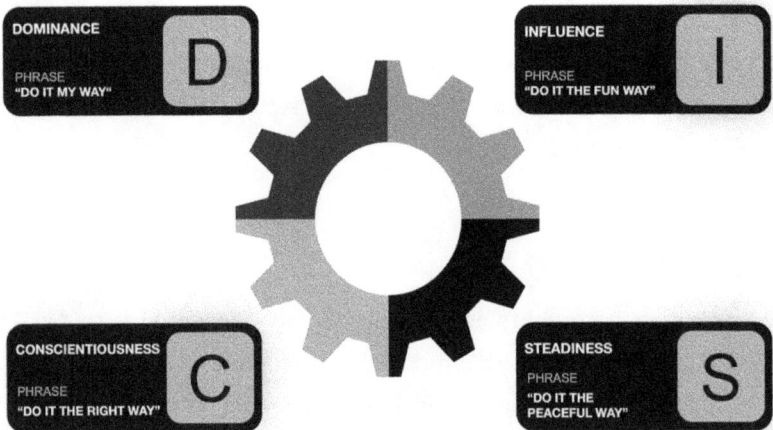

It's important to keep in mind that these four types are broad generalities and that any one person contains a mixture of them. However, once you become deeply familiar with DISC, it changes the way you understand, describe, and work with the people around you. It also changes your own understanding of what the organization needs from you as CEO.

Each of the four DISC personality types is effectively a different way to approach life. The Dominance type wants to win and deliver clear results. They like action a lot more than they like talk, and they admire people who share their ambitiousness.

The Influence type wants to be entertaining and have fun. They love to socialize and create connections and are motivated by public recognition of their successes.

The Steadiness type tries to ensure tranquility and harmony within the group. They highly value certainty and predictability, and employ careful thought before proceeding with action.

Finally, the Conscientiousness type likes to make sure things are done the right way and that the proper process is followed. They highly value organization and structure.

If you want to run an organization at scale, you will be required to balance the needs of all four types of people through your leadership style. Let's look at one example of how this plays out related to a key CEO responsibility: decision making.

DISC Types: Application

Let's say you're a strong Dominance personality, as many CEOs are. You pride yourself on your ability to take charge, make decisions, and show results. When making a major decision, such as a merger or acquisition or the need for layoffs, you tend to decide quickly, without much consultation, and expect people to move forward without delay.

I have strong D tendencies, and this was my process when I started my career. I would schedule a meeting to "discuss" the issue with only a few days' notice. I would go into the meeting with my decision already made, present the problem, outline my position, ask if there were any questions, and see if anybody expressed concerns. People would rarely speak up. This lack of objection would lead me to believe that there was general agreement and support for my decision. I would thus pronounce the decision final and go home feeling content that evening, looking forward to everyone quickly executing in the coming days.

I eventually learned that silence does not mean agreement—it was just that most of the people in the room weren't Dominance types like me. Steadiness and Conscientiousness personalities naturally tend to avoid confrontation, so they just weren't speaking up. The S personalities, who deeply value predictability and stability, may actually have been in a state of shock, thinking, "How could he possibly make this major decision without getting feedback from everyone involved? Did he think through what the repercussions would be?" The C personalities, who want to conscientiously follow established processes, would also have been in shock, thinking, "Wow, he made this decision without analyzing the data, without dotting the i's and crossing the t's. He didn't follow any sort of process! This is chaos!" Even the Influence personalities, the types who highly value relationships, might be offended. They are likely thinking, "He didn't ask what I thought about this personally . . . Guess my opinion isn't important!" Most of the team went home from those meetings thinking their CEO was either reckless, uncaring, or unsupportive. When everyone returned to work the next

Monday morning, instead of the decision being executed, there would be a lot of friction and grumbling about how the decision was made and communicated—with most of the tension rooted in our differing personalities.

I would notice this tension, of course. As a D type, my natural reaction was, "Wait a minute, don't they know I'm in charge? Don't they see that it's my job to make decisions? If they don't like the decision, tough!" The D leader may view the team as unsupportive or always pushing back on decisions.

Today, the decision-making process I use is quite different. Yes, I still make the high-level calls that affect the whole organization, but I do it in a way that brings along the I, S, and C types.

If you're a D personality as well, here's how you might handle the decision process so you don't end up in the boat I was in. Start a couple of weeks before you need to make the decision. Call a meeting of the executive team in which you lay out all the information relevant to the decision in a way that speaks to the non-D types. For the Conscientiousness personalities, you might say, "Here's the information I'm looking at in considering this decision. If you need additional information, you're welcome to go find it, and I would value your input, but this is everything I've got. You know everything I know. Do your analysis and figure out what you think we should do by Friday at one o'clock." For the Steadiness personalities, you need a different message: "Who are the other stakeholders we need input from? Who will be impacted by this decision? Go get input from those people and come prepared on Friday at one to talk about what you learned from these groups." And to the Influence personalities, you can say, "On Friday at one o'clock, I'd like you to spend five minutes making a case for what you think the decision should be, with clear evidence and direction as to why."

This isn't drastically different from how you would have prepared for the meeting before, but it's doing so in a way that brings all personality types into the fold. The other added benefit is that, by enlisting the help of your non-D peers, you could turn up useful perspectives. Even if you're going in with an idea of what you plan to decide, you will hopefully be self-aware and open-minded enough to consider additional information as it is presented. When everyone goes home that Friday afternoon after the meeting, they will all feel represented in the decision process. The Is will have had a chance to discuss it, the Ss to explain the broader impact on the organization, and the Cs to analyze and bring up pertinent details. Each was involved and each had their say. (We will discuss the importance of giving people a voice in decisions again in Responsibility 4, under the heading "Process Fairness.")

These are the types of tangible upgrades you can make to your leadership style once you understand DISC and other similar frameworks. Far from a dry exercise, learning about the different behavioral styles of your people leads to a more dynamic approach to the role of CEO.

USER MANUAL

Though personality assessments are useful, no out-of-the-box tool can ever fully capture all the dimensions of a human being's behavior and working style. That is why we recommend supplementing assessments with a User Manual—a short, self-authored document that describes how you operate and what you expect from your colleagues as CEO.

I came across the idea of a User Manual because of my own lack of self-awareness. In my early years as CEO, I would often be invited to various meetings within the organization. Halfway

THE PLATINUM RULE

You know the Golden Rule: Treat others as you would want to be treated. But when you are managing and leading people, you have to go beyond that. You have to follow the Platinum Rule: Treat others as *they* want to be treated. Because the people on your team all have very different personalities and working styles, maximizing their performance requires that you treat them according to these unique characteristics. This requires first learning about their characteristics, through tools like DISC and CliftonStrengths and through your own observation, and then tailoring your approach so it works for them. This not only gives your employees a better experience working for you; it also enables them to be significantly more productive.

through, I'd see that the team had the issue handled, so I'd get up and leave. To me, this was a sign of my full confidence in the team. In fact, if I had stayed, I thought I would have been usurping the manager's authority. But it eventually got back to me that my abrupt departures were unnerving people. *Why did the CEO just leave in the middle of a discussion? Is he upset? Does he not care?* Once I explained my intent, nobody had any problem with me getting up and leaving in the middle of a discussion, but for a while it had quite a few people concerned.

Eventually, I had collected a short list of my idiosyncrasies as a boss: I'm an email or in-person guy, not a phone guy. I don't naturally hand out profuse praise. I appreciate when people disagree with me. And I might just get up and leave during the meeting you invited me to. As the company grew, I found myself giving this same speech to all the new hires, particularly those on the executive team. So one day I typed up a document covering fifteen points I wanted people to know about me as a boss, ranging from how I communicate to what my basic expectations are of the people I manage. I called it "How to Be an Executive for Me."

Putting together this document not only reduced misunderstandings but also allowed me to better understand how I work, manage, and lead. (On page 40, you can see my full original document.) I later found that others, including the organizational psychologist Ben Dattner and strategist Ivar Kroghrud, have described this type of document as a "user's manual." This has become a practice we now recommend to all CEOs.

Following are a couple of guidelines to help you write your own User Manual. When you've got a draft, share it with your executive team. Ask if they have any feedback, as your User Manual may reflect distortions in your self-perception. Take any initial feedback you get and incorporate it if you feel it is accurate. Then revisit and revise your User Manual every six months or so, layering in any new discoveries about yourself and your management style. You may want to have two versions, one for executives that includes information about what you expect from those on the leadership team and another with more general information for the whole employee base.

As you write, remember that the User Manual isn't a device for making excuses. For example, I included in mine the fact that I don't naturally hand out profuse praise. I want people to know about that so they can come ask me if they have questions. But that *doesn't* mean that I can just never give praise. I need to be aware of this aspect of myself and throw more praise in the mix as I lead.

Writing Your User Manual

Your User Manual is a blueprint for working with you as CEO. In the User Manual, limit yourself to covering:

- **Your quirks, the things that make you unique.** Don't cover everything, just the handful of things that are distinctive to you. What makes you weird? (Don't worry, as the User Manual exercise reveals, *everyone* is weird.) Don't assign "good" or "bad" value judgments to anything—just tell people how you're different.

- **Items that are actionable.** Saying "I like to hear the truth" doesn't tell your colleagues much at all. Who doesn't like the truth? Make it more actionable: "If you see me doing something and think it could be done better, tell me. I value the chance to operate more effectively and will let you know if I disagree."

You may want to include insights from the assessments you've done. You could use CliftonStrengths language, for example, to write, "One of my strengths is Strategic, so when you bring something to me, expect me to ask a lot of 'what if' questions." Again, you want your whole team to speak a common language about how you work together, and a tool like CliftonStrengths can supply that.

It's also a good idea to have others write and share their own User Manuals. At companies I have led, we ask every employee to write one, and we then keep it where it's accessible to everyone on their team. This has proven to be an excellent way to grow understanding between very different types of people, alleviate harmful friction, and enrich the language people use to describe themselves and others.

USER MANUAL: JOEL TRAMMELL

1. I assume you know what you are doing unless proven otherwise. I won't hound you about details or constantly check on your progress. I think you are better at the job than I would be. I expect you, as an executive, to be autonomous and perform at a high level.

2. I don't hand out praise profusely (I am sure it has something to do with my childhood). If you don't feel you know how you are doing, you may want to ask. I will tell you. If I say you are doing great, I mean you are doing great, no BS.

3. This doesn't mean I don't pay attention to your performance. I will judge your performance in three fundamental ways:

   • your performance as a member of the executive team—we are going to run the company, not just me

   • your ability to attract and retain great talent in your organization

   • the performance of your department based on the metrics and goals that we agree are important for your success

4. I am highly competitive and expect to win in everything we do. Just because I don't run around yelling and screaming doesn't mean I am not passionate about the cause. I believe the race is a marathon, not a sprint, but I DO believe it is a race. I expect to see you compete and win.

5. I expect that you, as an executive, will be able to balance the concerns of shareholders, employees, and customers and not just represent the view of your department.

6. If you never disagree with me, you are not adding value. When you disagree, I need to hear your opinion.

7. I am busy, but that is not a reason for you not to engage me. Your performance is my number-ONE responsibility, so engage me whenever appropriate.

8. Don't complain to subordinates about other groups and how they do their job. It reflects poorly on you as an executive. Executives solve problems. If you have a complaint about another group, bring it to me immediately. If you think something can be done better, let me know now.

9. I don't need to be engaged if you are making a decision within your area of responsibility that won't sink the ship. If you want my opinion, I will give it, but don't feel the need to get approval within your scope.

10. I expect you to work for me if it is in your best interests to do so. It is my job to always make it in your best interests. If you find it is not in your best interests, please let me know. You don't owe me your loyalty. I will be happy to provide my honest opinion of what is best for your career.

11. If I leave during the middle of a discussion with you or your team, it is not because I don't care or am upset. It is because I don't believe I have anything to add, and I have confidence in you to solve the problem.

12. I am very direct in my conversation. Some people overreact to this style and try to read between the lines; there is no space between the lines. "I don't like the report" means "I don't like the report," not "I am about to fire you."

13. I prefer face-to-face communications. My second choice is email. My least favorite is phone. I like being able to confirm visually that I am understanding what you are saying.

14. Be simple and clear in communications. If you need me to make a decision, call it out. Don't make me read a novel to figure out the punchline. Give me the punchline, and then include the novel if you like.

15. I favor action over strategy; do something even if it is wrong. Fail fast and then correct course.

THE WELL-ROUNDED CEO

We mentioned earlier that focusing on a person's strengths—as the CliftonStrengths methodology encourages—is a good way to help that person excel. The idea is that leaning into your natural strengths will get you further than trying to patch up your weaknesses.

This is very true for individual contributors. If you're a brilliant strategic thinker, you can seek out roles where you can apply that proclivity and not worry too much about the tactical, execution-oriented side of the equation. Or if you're a brilliant software engineer, you can hone those skills and excel without fully developing your people skills.

For the CEO, the picture is different. Most CEOs moved up in the organization because of their strength in a particular area. If they were a salesperson or a technologist or a financial expert and a strong D personality, they focused on results in their domain. That likely got them promoted, then promoted again. This past success will lead them to think, "Well, focusing on results is what makes me special, what makes me so good at my job. So as CEO, I'm going to focus on results!" But this leads to a lopsided approach.

Whereas a specialist can lean into a small set of strengths, the CEO role calls for a generalist. The higher you rise in management, the more you need to cover all your bases. You can't be dominant *or* influential *or* steady *or* conscientious. You must be all these things, to some degree, at once. It's no longer about being personally successful—now it's about making your team successful, and that requires a mix.

If you're a Dominance leader, you'll need to learn how to connect with and persuade other people in the organization (Influence), to make sure the team feels confident and secure

AN ASYMMETRICAL RELATIONSHIP

One peculiarity of the boss-employee relationship is the out-sized, one-way impact the boss has on the employee's life. Think back to your first job. Your boss was likely the first or second most impactful person in your life at the time. You probably spent more time around them than you did with your family. Your relationship with the boss determined how well you could provide for yourself (and others), where you could live, and whether your time at work was rewarding or miserable. Yet to the boss, you were just one among a whole team of employees.

When you become the CEO, this dynamic grows even more intense. As chief executive of your organization, you will likely be one of the most impactful people in the lives of your direct reports. Yet the relationship is asymmetrical: You have many direct reports, a board, other employees you interact with, and of course your family and friends. You may be number two in their life while they are somewhere in the twenties or thirties for you. This can result in an executive valuing your time, your input, and your comments more than you appear to value them. CEOs must maintain awareness of this dynamic and strive to treat the people on their team with the same level of interest and respect that is afforded to them.

CEOs must also be aware of the bubble that their title puts them in. Because people do see you as so impactful in their lives, you may have a harder time getting to their real feelings, at least until you build up trust with them. We will discuss this more in Part III, in the section about the CEO skill of awareness.

(Steadiness), and to make sure you do the necessary homework and have good processes in place (Conscientiousness). The larger your team gets, and the broader the responsibilities, the less you will be able to focus on just one strength or aspect of your personality. By the time you reach CEO, you're called upon to integrate a variety of types and strengths into how you lead. This requires intention and effort. It's easier to keep falling back on your natural proclivities, but if you do, you will have limited leadership impact across the organization.

Additionally, organizations can easily become unbalanced in the four areas related to DISC. As CEO, it is your job to understand where the organization is currently, and what it needs moving forward. For example, if you take over from a leader who was very inspiring and fun-loving, the company may be weak in process and attention to detail. If this is not your natural style, it will be important for you to augment your style through people or process: either hire people who naturally focus on this area or implement processes to force more attention into this area. Typically a CEO is naturally going to be good at one of the four dimensions of leadership—Dominance, Influence, Steadiness, and Conscientiousness—so it's important for the CEO to understand which is their default, where they need to improve, and what adjustments their particular organization needs to achieve a balanced approach.

BECOMING FLUENT IN THE LANGUAGE OF PEOPLE: BUILD YOUR PLAYBOOK

- **Take the DISC and StrengthsFinder assessments, and have your executive team do the same.** Hold a meeting to discuss the results. Are there any surprises? What trends do you observe across the team?

- **Write your User Manual.** Share the things that make you unique, including your quirks, your leadership style, and your expectations of the people who work for you. Encourage your executives to write their own User Manuals. Hold a meeting where everyone on the team discusses the top two or three items from their User Manual.

- **Roll out assessments and User Manuals across the organization.** Encourage all managers to take DISC and CliftonStrengths assessments, write their User Manuals, and have their employees do the same. Communicate abundantly about the purpose of these tools: for managers in the organization to understand themselves and their employees as unique individuals, and for employees to collaborate more productively throughout the company.

MOTIVATORS & AGGRAVATORS

We have established that past the startup phase, the CEO delivers work *through* other people. But how do you motivate those people to do the things you believe need to be done? Yell orders? Be really charming? Pay a lot?

None of those methods work sustainably. Better is to understand and apply a simple theory of motivation in your workplace. The one we'll cover in this chapter was proposed decades ago and has been repeatedly proven in practice, yet most CEOs don't understand the valuable lessons it holds.

WHY DO PEOPLE COME TO WORK?

When you ask someone what motivates people at work, the almost universal first answer you hear is "Money." It's true: In some situations, money can be a motivator at work. It's just that this is not the case for most knowledge workers in the United

States. Unlike in a developing country, your employees have their basic survival needs met and thus require a lot more than a paycheck to be productively engaged at work. Money is the minimum requirement to get them to show up, but it doesn't ensure they're going to perform once they get there.

So, if money is not the primary motivator, what is? Why do people take jobs and stay engaged in organizations? Many experts have pursued this question over the years. The American psychologist Frederick Herzberg summarized his work on the topic in a *Harvard Business Review* article titled "One More Time: How Do You Motivate Employees?" Last time we looked, it was the most reprinted article in the history of the magazine. This is likely because, beginning in the 1960s, Herzberg identified a highly useful model for thinking about the factors that influence a person's motivation to put in effort at their job. Herzberg proved his model through various applications, and interestingly, the factors he identified over fifty years ago remain virtually unchanged today. His original article is an eye-opening distillation of his career's work, and we recommend you read it. Here, we will summarize Herzberg's key findings and examine how they relate to the CEO role.

Herzberg's model, known as *two-factor theory*, proposes two sets of factors in the workplace, one of which encourages motivation and the other of which causes demotivation. The demotivating factors are the **aggravators** (Herzberg called them "hygiene factors," but we use this more descriptive term). These factors are what people complain about and cause problems at work. The other factors are the **motivators**, the things that influence employees to come to work and put in discretionary effort. Importantly, Herzberg noted that these two sets of factors operate independently of one another. This means that taking away aggravators is not enough to motivate people in the absence of true motivating factors. It also means that aggravators are still going to bug people even when you have motivating factors in place. Herzberg found that when you ask people what contributes to their job satisfaction, they almost always mention motivators, while if you ask them what dissatisfies them about the job, you'll most often hear about aggravators.

Distinguishing aggravators from motivators is important if the CEO wants to operate with an effective model for motivating employees. We will begin by looking at the motivators and how the CEO might enhance them.

MOTIVATORS

In my career, I've conducted over one thousand job interviews. Talking to that many people really deepened my understanding of how people think about their jobs. One question I liked to ask was: "What was your best day of work so far?" Almost without fail, the candidate would tell me a story about when they and their team achieved something that didn't at first seem possible. Or I'd hear about the day that they and their team were *recognized* for making such an achievement. It's no surprise, then, that Herzberg identified the top two motivators in the workplace as **achievement** and **recognition**. These two clearly go hand in hand: people enjoy the feeling of accomplishing something great, and they also want to be recognized for it. These drives are wired into us at a deep level.

How do CEOs get in the way of achievement as a motivator? The most common way is simply not defining what is to be achieved. Imagine playing a football game with no end zones and no scoreboard. How motivated are players going to be with no idea how to score? Not very, of course. Yet that is the situation many CEOs create by failing to articulate clear, achievable, relevant objectives. They just put their people out on the field and say, "Run as hard as you can! Give it your all!" To support achievement as a motivator, you will need to create clear objectives at the corporate level, then help drive goal setting through all levels of the organization. We often say that **"goals give meaning to tasks."** By this we mean that each individual needs to understand what they're trying to achieve and why; only then will the daily work that goes into the goal feel meaningful. We'll discuss how to set goals and objectives well in Part II of this book.

Once an achievement is made by the team, you can enhance that motivator with its partner: recognition. CEO time is well-spent on ensuring that people feel seen and appreciated when they contribute to the company's successes. The challenge is that while every employee wants to be recognized, they often want to be recognized in different ways. Here the personality variations we discussed in the previous chapter come into play. Someone with an Influence personality would likely be highly motivated by being called up on stage, given a plaque, and maybe allowed to say a few words. But for a Steadiness or Conscientiousness personality, such public recognition would be anathema. Remember the Platinum Rule: Everyone needs to be recognized in a way that is most fulfilling for them. For other personalities, personal touches like a handwritten thank-you note or a gift card to their favorite restaurant might be most meaningful. Still other people may feel most recognized by a couple of extra vacation days or a chance to attend a seminar or conference on the company dime.

Next on the list of motivators is the **work itself**. For many people, the actual content of the job can be deeply motivating, especially when it fits their interests, passions, and what they want to do in life. In some jobs, the motivation inherent in the work is clear: If you hire a master woodworker at your woodworking shop, you know they likely get a lot of intrinsic reward from crafting wood. But with knowledge workers, things get complicated. In a typical knowledge job, there will be aspects the employee finds rewarding and other aspects they don't. One of your roles as CEO is rearranging responsibilities so the people working for you can spend more time engaged in tasks that are rewarding and energizing to them and less time with unappealing tasks. Yes, unappealing tasks are sometimes necessary. However, what's unappealing to one person may be engaging to another. We have extensively used CliftonStrengths to figure out how to structure roles in the organization so that people can use their strengths and preferences as much as possible.

Number four on the list of motivators is **responsibility**. When someone feels real ownership over a process or outcome, they are usually more motivated to do the work required. When they have responsibility, the employee feels they have greater control and more room to innovate, which often leads to better outcomes anyway. We encourage CEOs to ensure that each employee in the organization has a defined list of responsibilities. This is very different from a task list. The employee's responsibilities answer the question "What do you *own* in the organization?" Working with the employee to create ownership over those items is a great way to enhance this motivator.

Finally, number five on the list of motivators is the **opportunity for advancement and growth**. For top performers, I might even move this to the number-three spot. Most people want to progress in their field, and they typically don't take jobs at the same level as the one they had before. If somebody calls you up and says, "I've got the perfect job for you. You're going to do exactly what you're doing now, make exactly the same money you're making now, except you're going to do it in the building across the street," most people would not be motivated to take that job. People take on jobs because they are bigger, better, and more challenging than what they had previously. They want to move their career forward. In your organization, employees—especially top talent—should be nurtured in this pursuit of new skills, professional growth, and career advancement.

The best way for CEOs to maximize this motivator is through continuous coaching relationships. In addition to offering coaching to your own direct reports, you must build the coaching capability of each manager in your organization. We will discuss this later on in the book.

AGGRAVATORS

Now to the other side of the motivation equation: the aggravators. These are the factors that get in the way of good work, the things employees feel they shouldn't have to worry about in the first place. When you remove one, the aggravation is reduced, but motivation isn't necessarily improved.

The number-one item on the list of aggravators is **company policies**, specifically the bad ones. These are the stupid rules that might have had a purpose at one point but now just cause grief for the organization. As CEO, you are probably not even aware of many of these bad policies because you are exempt or far removed from how they are applied for the people who work at your company.

You can see a classic example of this in the show *Undercover*

Boss, which documents CEOs as they are shocked by the obstacles their own frontline employees face. We recommend you try to find out about these policies before they do further damage. When I took over as CEO of a public company, it had executed over one hundred acquisitions in years prior, and I knew that between that and its forty-year existence, there had to be some bad policies in place. On my first day, I hosted a call with the more than five hundred managers in the organization and said, "I know we have some outdated policies and procedures in this organization, and as CEO, I'm responsible for all of them." I explained that I would never experience the vast majority of them personally, but that it was important to remove the ones that no longer served us. Sure enough, managers and employees across the company had no trouble pinpointing aggravating red tape, and I did everything possible to empower them to remove it.

Most companies make policy decisions because of a negative occurrence, and these policies can live on well past their usefulness. For example, if someone wrecks a rental car on a business trip, the company might require driver training for all employees renting a car in the future. This generalizes one unfortunate event to everyone and places an undue burden on all the employees who have never wrecked a car on a business trip. If these kinds of policies pile up like a geological record of past mistakes, the whole organization will end up slower and more aggravated.

The second item on the aggravator list is **supervision**—in other words, how an employee's boss manages them. We all have bad-manager stories. One of the worst I heard was about a call center of over one hundred salespeople, all smiling and dialing for dollars in a cube farm. Unfortunately, the company had begun to struggle. In an act that deserves the Worst Manager Ever award, the group's manager decided to install elevated platforms—like deer stands—above the cubes. This way, the bosses could sit in the stands, observe the salespeople, and make sure they were giving their best effort. Obviously, that did not lead to improved performance, but it *did* lead to many of the top salespeople immediately quitting. That's an extreme example, but the way in which employees are supervised can cause major aggravation. As they say, people don't leave companies; they leave managers. Taking down the deer stand won't create motivation, but it could just aggravate your best people out the door.

Supervision is tightly linked to the next aggravator on the list: **the employee's relationship with the supervisor**. Everyone expects their boss to be a decent person. They don't expect to be best buddies, but they do expect them to be a decent, honorable human being. If an employee considers their boss untrustworthy or unreliable, or if boss and employee are constantly clashing, that can be a big aggravator. One way to clear up this aggravator is to have managers become fluent in a language like DISC. As we saw before, the majority of interpersonal tension in the workplace is based in two people's failure to understand each other's personality and working style.

The fourth aggravator is **work conditions**. Think of Milton from *Office Space*, deprived of his red stapler and getting moved down to Storage B, a.k.a. the basement. Under conditions like that, the employee will clearly be aggravated. Back when Herzberg was doing his work on motivation, the average employee's working conditions were comparatively worse than the ergonomic, tech-enhanced environments we have today. But it's all relative, and there are still many ways your employees may be aggravated by work conditions. It could be anything from a slow laptop to a perpetually freezing office. Work-from-home has introduced a whole new set of this type of aggravator, including technical difficulties, noise and distractions, and challenging family situations. These are, of course, not all controllable by the CEO or the HR department. However, it is your responsibility to ensure that all employees have space and equipment that at least meets minimum requirements to work comfortably.

Number five on the list of aggravators is **salary**. How is salary an aggravator? Because perceived unfair pay is something that contributes significantly to job dissatisfaction, but after you reach a point where the person believes they are paid fairly, salary does not create intrinsic motivation.

We can tell you from long experience that pay fairness is all about the employee's perception. For many people, it's a subjective judgment based upon their past experiences; for others it's relative to what others in the organization make; for yet others, their idea of fairness is based on what peers across the industry make. To increase perceptions of fairness, we recommend setting salaries with as much objectivity as possible. If you can show the employee that they are paid at least the broader market rate for roles similar to theirs, salary is unlikely to be an aggravator for them. But this won't be the case if you, for example, allow certain employees to negotiate a considerably higher salary while paying their peers in comparable roles, with comparable experience and qualifications, the market rate. Once that is discovered, salary will crop up as a significant aggravator.

Along similar lines, monetary incentives and pay-for-performance schemes almost always fail to create lasting motivation (which we would expect, since pay is an aggravator). Several years ago I attended a conference where *Good to Great* author Jim Collins was a keynote speaker. Someone asked him at the end of his presentation what he thought about incentive compensation. In the great companies he studied, did paying people for performance make a difference? Jim got very animated, started pounding the table, and said, "You cannot turn the wrong people into the right people with money." He repeated it three times. He then went on to explain that the purpose of a pay system in an organization is to retain good people who wake up every day wanting to do great things. You cannot, Jim said, create those people through an incentive pay structure.

Consider also the fact that pay-for-performance does not actually exist in the corporate world. If it did, we would have huge variations in pay for people doing similar jobs, and that is just not tenable. The only place where you truly see pay-for-performance is in major league sports, and even that—for most sports—is pay for past performance. You get paid on how great a year you had last year, which may not be an accurate representation of your performance this year. Only in the true prize-money sports like golf or tennis is there a direct correlation between your pay and your score in each tournament. And in those situations, the top performers usually make an extreme amount of money, while the rest barely get by. The tournament format may be easily measurable, but for most jobs in most organizations, performance cannot be measured in that same objective way.

The final aggravator is the employee's **relationship with peers**. As we expect of our boss, most of us expect that the people we work with will be reasonably decent human beings. If we perceive that even one of them isn't, our dissatisfaction with the job can grow. Famously, Robert Sutton wrote *The No Asshole Rule*, in which he encouraged organizations not to put up with people who were real troublemakers. Sutton correctly saw that dysfunctional peer relationships in the organization cause more than just surface-level issues.

REMOVING AGGRAVATORS, ENHANCING MOTIVATORS

As CEO, you are ultimately responsible for the motivators and aggravators your workforce experiences at work. It bears repeating: Don't think that you can inspire lasting motivation by focusing only on the aggravators. Your work with the management team to remove aggravators should be paired with concerted attention to enhancing the motivators. These are separate issues that must be addressed through different actions.

MOTIVATORS	AGGRAVATORS
Achievement	Company Policy
Recognition	Supervision
Work Itself	Relationship with Supervisor
Responsibility	Work Conditions
Opportunity for Advancement and Growth	Salary
	Relationship with Peers

When you put the lists of motivators and aggravators side by side, as in the table on the previous page, there are interesting observations to be made. On the **aggravator side,** notice that your typical mid-level manager likely needs help from the top of the organization to affect change. They probably cannot set company policy or control work conditions, and probably aren't the ultimate authority on establishing salary either. This means that your role as CEO requires engaging the whole management team—not just your direct reports—in identifying aggravators in the company and then doing something about them. (Even the two aggravators that are in control of the manager, supervision and relationship with supervisor, are something the CEO should take great interest in. If you have a bad apple among your executive, mid-level, or frontline managers, it's something you should be aware of—and address.)

On the other hand, the five items on the **motivator side** are usually in direct control of a manager. If a manager comes to the CEO and says, "My team just isn't motivated," the CEO can often conclude that the locus of the issue is the manager themselves. Certainly, CEOs can lay fertile ground for motivation, but **direct managers have the primary impact on motivators**. There is plenty of proof for this. Gallup has gathered data on employee engagement across thousands of companies and found that employee engagement varies dramatically from department to department based upon the manager and management team in that particular area. They conclude that about 70 percent of variance in employee engagement is due to the direct manager.

So, as CEO, your action plan for creating a broadly motivated team should include: (a) close attention to how the organization as a whole can clear away aggravators for employees at all levels, and (b) education and empowerment of managers around the motivators, so they can enhance these factors for each person in the teams they lead.

MOTIVATORS & AGGRAVATORS: BUILD YOUR PLAYBOOK

- **Discuss the list of motivators and aggravators with your executive team.** Think through each one and write down an action you and/or other leaders in the organization can take to reinforce the motivators and remove the aggravators.

- **Request feedback from every manager in the company regarding the aggravators.** While managers can often reinforce the motivators themselves, they may need organizational support to address aggravators. Thank managers for the feedback they give, and either act on it or explain why you are not acting on it right now.

THE 3 TOOLS
OF THE CEO

S o far in the Chief Executive Operating System, we've seen that your organization consists of a group of humans organized into six different functions of the business. All of those humans have their own unique strengths, working styles, and personalities. And all of them are affected by various aggravators and motivators that determine their engagement in the mission of your organization. If the CEO wants to be effective, they must understand these people-related dynamics.

But now we arrive at the next question: How does the CEO get this diverse, multifaceted group of people to actually do the right stuff?

It's a seductive idea to think that because you're CEO, you have all the power and can thus easily effect change in the organization. But in practice, CEOs find that their power is quite limited. You can give people commands all day, but it doesn't mean people will follow them. You can deliver an inspiring speech, but it doesn't mean employees will internalize the message. And you can fire someone, but did that really help? Now you've just got to find someone new.

To actually have the desired effect on the organization, the CEO must answer three basic questions that correspond with three distinct tools every CEO has at their disposal:

- **Management—What needs to be done?** The CEO uses the management tool when **making decisions about those things they control because of their position in the organization.** You are managing when you place people in certain roles, define their responsibilities, establish company objectives, and allocate resources.

- **Leadership—Why should we do it?** The CEO uses the leadership tool when **influencing the organization to willingly follow their direction.** Dwight D. Eisenhower defined leadership perfectly, saying that it is "the art of getting someone else to do something you want done because they want to do it."

- **Coaching—How can we do it best?** The CEO uses the coaching tool when **interactively enabling the development of employees** and helping them grow their abilities. Most CEOs do the majority of their coaching with direct reports on the executive team, but they also need to ensure that every manager in the organization is an effective coach—someone able to work one-on-one with their direct reports to grow their skills.

Each tool is a mode the CEO can operate in. To be effective, the CEO must master all three of these tools, knowing when to use each and how to balance them against each other. Let's briefly look at what they look like in practice.

Management
What to do

Leadership
Why to do it

Coaching
How to do it

MANAGING: ANSWERING THE WHAT

We define the management tool of the CEO as *making decisions about the things you control because of your position*. Because you are chief executive, those decisions involve the most consequential issues facing the organization: What objectives are we striving toward? Who holds which roles, and what are their responsibilities? How do we best allocate capital and human talent in support of our shared objectives? At times, the management decisions you're called upon to make can be exciting and forward-looking, such as making a big acquisition. At other times, they're choices you would rather avoid, such as doing a layoff or shutting down an unsuccessful project.

As you can see from the definition above, the management tool is rooted in strong decision making. This is a topic we will cover in more depth in later sections of the book. For now, just understand that the CEO must treat management decisions with great care, as they define the very essence of *what* the organization is doing. In making management decisions, the CEO must consider all the complex human dynamics we have discussed up to this point. For example, setting the organization's compensation strategy is a fundamental management decision; if the CEO doesn't understand how salary can function as an aggravator, they may make a decision that has considerable negative outcomes across the workforce.

While it may not seem as glamorous, the management tool is every bit as vital as the leadership tool. In today's business press, you see a lot of denigration of management and raising up of leadership, as if leadership is the superior mode on a spectrum. We disagree. Management and leadership are distinct and equally important tools. Overreliance on one at the expense of the other creates an imbalance in the CEO's approach. As the author and academic Henry Mintzberg once said, "Managers who don't lead are quite discouraging, but leaders who don't manage don't know what's going on." You do need to inspire people through leadership, as we'll discuss momentarily, but this must be backed up by clear, well-thought-out management decisions.

There are several mistakes CEOs can make with the management tool. The most common is pronouncing a decision and expecting people to go execute without providing them the *why* or the *how*. This is why CEOs must use the management tool in conjunction with leadership (*why*) and coaching (*how*). Another common mistake is delaying too long in making management decisions. If you are dragging your feet on high-level decisions, you are having a huge impact on the organization as they wait around for you to make a move—and very little may be getting done in the meantime. A third mistake with the management tool is not being precise enough about what needs to be done, thereby leaving employees guessing, wondering, or having to discover what needs to be done through trial and error. It is important, particularly as an organization grows in size, that management decisions are captured, recorded, and communicated to the appropriate people in the organization.

LEADING: ANSWERING THE WHY

If management is about the decisions you make because of your authority as CEO, leadership is *the ability to influence others to willingly follow your direction.* Leadership shows people *why* they should engage with the mission and objectives you have established for the company—as eagerly as if it were their own idea—and what they're going to get out of it. This is the essence of Eisenhower's definition of leadership quoted earlier: "getting someone else to do something you want done because they want to do it." The challenge, of course, is knowing how to put this paradoxical idea into practice.

Eisenhower famously convinced a group of young soldiers to storm a beach while knowing that many of them would not return. Clearly, he exhibited leadership in that endeavor, but what did he actually do? Most of those troops would never have personally met Eisenhower. In those days, communication was limited to phone or black-and-white film. Many of the soldiers would not even have heard Eisenhower speak in person. What motivated those individuals was, in large part, Eisenhower's reputation within the military as a great leader. He had mastered the art of influence to the degree that his leadership moved even those with whom he had not had direct contact.

As CEO, you have a similar challenge. How do you provide leadership when you can't have a personal relationship with everyone in the organization? How do you build the sort of influence that encourages people to bring their own personal enthusiasm to the mission of the company? The most consistent way is to exhibit three core characteristics that we call the three Cs of leadership. They are as follows.

Credibility. When a leader speaks, it is vitally important that everyone believes that the information they share is true to the best of the leader's knowledge. To maintain this *credibility*, you must tell the truth 100 percent of the time. Just one slip-up, where you are perceived to have misrepresented or hid information, is enough to permanently destroy your credibility.

Credibility often becomes a problem when leaders want to convince others (and maybe even themselves) that things at the company are going better than they actually are. They fall into the trap of becoming a company cheerleader. In doing so, they fail to confront objective reality and admit when things are less than ideal. Of course, eventually the truth becomes apparent, and the leader's credibility is shot. You do not have to be an Eeyore about the company's prospects, but you do owe your employees the truth. To display real credibility, it is not enough to simply *not* lie—you have to proactively communicate any information that impacts employees or their jobs. In Part III, we will talk further about the CEO skill of communicating authentically and transparently. It's central to building your credibility.

Competence. The second of the characteristics you need to display if you want to build your leadership influence is *competence*. People want leaders who are knowledgeable about the business and who show proficiency in their domains. As CEO, this means you should have a handle on the fundamentals of the six areas of the business we discussed earlier in this section ("Triangles of Tension"), and that you must master the five responsibilities we will discuss next. However, competence does not mean you have to know everything about every part of the business. In fact, "I don't know" is one of the most powerful phrases in the CEO's vocabulary. As long as you demonstrate competence where you have it, admitting you don't know something builds that first C, credibility.

Clearly, there is a balance here. Pleading ignorance all the time will cause employees to doubt your competence. But there will be many days where you just don't have an answer in the moment. You will actually display more competence if you admit this. Same goes for when you have made a mistake. The faster you recognize your own mistakes and change direction, the more positively you will be viewed. Nothing destroys a leader's aura of competence more than making a mistake and being unwilling to acknowledge it, even though it's obvious to everyone else in the organization.

Caring. The third C of leadership is *caring*. This may be the hardest for many driven leaders to exhibit. Do people believe that you will put their interests on the same level as your own interests, all for the greater good of the organization? Do they believe that "We are all in this together"? Or do they believe you're looking out for yourself above all? I think the military axiom that "troops eat first; leaders eat last" is very appropriate to the discussion of caring. Many CEOs destroy the natural goodwill of employees by establishing perks for themselves and their executives. Things like the reserved parking spots, the exclusive executive cafeteria, and the first-class business travel can destroy any sense that you actually care about employees at all levels of the organization. Pay close attention to what you convey, because people are always watching your behavior. Something as simple as passing an employee in the hallway can take on huge significance if that employee doesn't interact with you often. Their opinion of you—and how much you actually care—is likely to be formed in brief encounters like these. Your ability to engage and make them feel special can go a long way.

When I was still in high school, I went to visit my brother at his job site, a paper mill in DeRidder, Louisiana. While I knew he worked as an engineer, I had little idea what an engineer did at a paper mill. He took me on a tour of the massive plant. It was both interesting and a little scary. Climbing up on the top of a cooling tower was not exactly my cup of tea. But the strongest memory forty years later is the plant manager inviting us into his office and spending time visiting with us. He talked about what a great job my brother was doing. It was obvious he cared about his employees. My brother was one of probably a thousand people who worked at that plant. I'm sure the plant manager could have found other things to do than talk to a high school kid, but those few minutes he took had a big impact on both my brother and me.

When hard times come, you have notable opportunities to demonstrate your caring. CEOs have a bad reputation, often deserved, because of the golden parachutes they take—leaving the employees to clean up the pieces. Since you're likely to be the most highly compensated person in the organization, especially if things go well, you should also be willing to take a significant downside risk when things go poorly. For example, anytime I had a situation that required cutting salaries, I always cut my own salary by a much bigger percentage than the others. I wanted people to know that I cared, and that I didn't place my personal interests ahead of theirs.

Some CEOs struggle with caring too much and it causes them to constantly beat themselves up about the business. This is not healthy either. Like so many aspects of the CEO role, this one requires a proper balance. People don't expect you to go down with the ship, but they do expect you to be the last person on the lifeboat, and to make sure that everyone has been taken care of before you abandon ship.

As you work to build the three Cs, understand that leadership happens in the eye of the person being led. **You may feel that you are credible, competent, and caring, but what matters is how employees perceive and interpret your behavior.** You can be the most caring person in the world, but if employees don't experience that from you, they will not follow your leadership. A great example is recent American politics. There are millions of people in the country who, if former President Obama called them up on the telephone today and said, "Hey,

I've got this project I want you to support," would jump at the chance to follow his lead. There is another group of millions who, if former President Trump called them up with the same offer, would also jump at that chance. Now, you could easily point out areas in which both individuals violated credibility, competence, and caring in the eyes of many. But the followers of both men don't see it that way; they perceive their person as having the three Cs.

What can you do about this reality? When it comes to the three Cs, don't just work on your internal states. Think long and hard about how you can *demonstrate* your credibility, competence, and caring through actions. In any organization, people will generally give you the benefit of the doubt as the CEO. Some percentage will follow you stalwartly just because of your position no matter what. Another, usually small, percentage will be those who are not trusting by nature and might hold out against being led despite your best efforts. For the rest, it is up to you to influence them to willingly follow your direction by practicing the three Cs. A good CEO should be able to get there with 80 to 90 percent of the employees in the organization.

COACHING: ANSWERING THE HOW

The third tool of the CEO, to be used in conjunction with managing and leading, is coaching. We define coaching as an *interactive process for enabling the development of employees.* As discussed earlier, one of the key motivators for employees is the ability to advance and grow in their role, particularly for the top performers. For this reason, every manager in a company should be in a coaching relationship with all of their direct reports.

Unfortunately, many CEOs spend a lot more time telling their employees *what* to do (management) than helping them discover *how* to do it best (coaching).

For the CEO, you may ask, "How can I be a coach to executives who know far more about doing their job than I do?" Being in a coaching relationship does not require you to be an expert in the technical aspects of a particular job. Bill Belichick, head coach of the New England Patriots, is a lock for the Hall of Fame and will probably go down as the greatest coach in the history of the NFL. What position did Belichick play? None. He never played football in the NFL! Belichick is not an expert at any position from a technical aspect. But he *is* an expert at setting a clear direction and helping players see whether they are accomplishing the appropriate goals and objectives for their individual positions.

Good CEOs have a similar dynamic with their direct reports. There's a simple four-step process that you can engage in to coach any individual. The process starts by *establishing trust* with the person. It is really hard to change anybody's behavior until you have a trusted relationship with that person. That happens over the days, weeks, and months you work with them and especially as you demonstrate the three Cs. Don't assume that the executive will automatically trust your intentions in coaching them. You must demonstrate that they can trust you, through your words and actions. Only then will they be interested in benefiting from the coaching you can provide. John Maxwell put it eloquently when he said, "People don't care how much you know until they know how much you care."

Once you have built trust, the second stage in the coaching process is to *make it personal.* Make sure you understand the person's individual goals and ambitions and that you're tailoring your coaching to their personality, remembering the Platinum

Rule. For a long time in my career, I thought everyone wanted to be CEO and they just hadn't gotten there yet, especially the executives on my team. It turns out that's not true, of course. Many people are happy to be CFO, head of sales, or another executive role. I wasn't an effective coach to them because I hadn't learned about their personal career ambitions.

Once you understand where that person wants to go in their career, then your third step as coach is to *commit to growth*. Your best executives will be on a journey of growth over their entire career. As you coach, show your commitment to helping them along this growth journey. Ask questions that peel back the layers to reveal their desired path. Help them set concrete growth goals that get them further down that path. What skills do they want to develop? What kind of feedback is important to them? What types of people do they need to connect with? What resources can you connect them with?

The fourth and arguably most critical step of the coaching process is *ensuring accountability* to the growth goals established in the previous step. It is easy to fall into comfortable amnesia between coaching sessions and let goals slip. It takes more effort to take good notes, remember what the employee is trying to achieve, and ensure that real, meaningful steps are being taken. Unless you show this discipline with your coaching conversations, you cannot expect discipline from the executive in carrying out a growth plan. As we will discuss more in Part III, accountability is ultimately about forcing the person to face objective reality, even when that reality is not ideal. You must do this in the coaching process, providing an independent view of how the employee is progressing—or not progressing—toward their development goals.

Some CEOs worry that they will coach a great executive

out of the organization. This reminds me of a poster I have in my office that documents a conversation between a CFO and CEO. The CFO comes in and says, "What if we train all these people and they leave?" The CEO replies, "What if we don't and they stay?" That concept is critical to being successful as CEO. You have to constantly develop people throughout the organization to drive performance and retention. This includes your executives. Especially if your organization is growing, your executives can develop extensively within the company for many years. A company growing at 25 percent will double in size in three years, allowing for executives to take on constantly changing roles and responsibilities. That growth will also open additional management opportunities within your organization for other top performers.

Another reason coaching is so important is that many, possibly most, of your people will be inexperienced in their current role. When I was running NetQoS, the network performance company I founded in 2000 with my wife, we often hired and promoted people into roles that were a significant step up from their previous role. Why didn't I just hire all seasoned leaders into our fast-growing startup? In general, high-performing people do not want to take a job they have already experienced. They want a new job that is bigger, broader, or more impactful than their previous job. This is human nature; as we have discussed, people want to feel that they are advancing in their career. And in most cases, a CEO of a growing business is better off hiring talented, ambitious people into roles that will challenge them than they would be hiring people who meet a long, perfect checklist of experience. Hiring for growth prevents stagnation and keeps motivation high. But it also means that you will be running an organization with a bunch of people who are inexperienced. Thus, your organization should be broadly committed to continuous development, and every manager working there should also be trained in how to coach their own employees. And it all starts with your example and the one-on-one coaching you provide to your own direct reports, no matter how brilliant and far along in their careers they are.

WHEN TO USE WHICH TOOL

The three tools of the CEO are management, leadership, and coaching, and they should be used in about equal measure for best results. In some situations, you may be unsure which tool is appropriate. Ask yourself the following questions to determine your best option.

- Does the organization/group/individual understand **what** to do? If not, use the management tool. Use your authority as CEO to make clear decisions on the best course of action. Show people what the priorities are.

- Does the organization/group/individual understand **why** they should do it? If not, use the leadership tool. Relying on the influence you've built by demonstrating the three Cs, explain what's at stake in the mission and what's in it for each member of the team.

- Does the employee understand **how** to do it? If not, use the coaching tool. Engage in the four-step coaching process with your direct reports, and require that all managers in the organization provide coaching to their own employees.

THE 3 TOOLS OF THE CEO: BUILD YOUR PLAYBOOK

- **In the next 1-on-1 with each of your direct reports, review their goals through the lens of *what* they need to do, *why* they need to do it, and whether they know *how* to do it.** If any of these areas is unclear, understand that you will need to use the management, leadership, or coaching tool, respectively, going forward.

PART II
EXECUTION

As we saw in Part I, the first and foundational part of the Chief Executive Operating System is **PEOPLE**. Your operating system must include an understanding of how the people your organization serves are grouped into six areas (Triangles of Tension); familiarity with personality types and a language to describe the rich variation among them; mastery of a model for motivating people; and facility with the your three essential tools in accomplishing success through others—management, leadership, and coaching.

Moving to Part II of the Chief Executive Operating System, we arrive at **EXECUTION**. This aspect of the job is central enough to be right there in the middle of your title. In my first book, *The CEO Tightrope*, I discussed the five core responsibilities that enable CEOs to execute effectively, and they inform the substance of this part of the Chief Executive Operating System. In the following chapters, we will look at how these responsibilities guide what the CEO actually does day in and day out.

As CEO, you are the one person in the organization with full autonomy over what you work on every day. In some ways this can be very freeing, but it can also lead to unhealthy habits. Many CEOs launch into each day looking for the biggest problem and spend most of their time playing whack-a-mole. This is a short-sighted approach to the job that certainly does not deliver predictable long-term results. In contrast, understanding the five responsibilities offers you a systematic guide to how best to spend your time as CEO.

For deeper dives into each responsibility, particularly the balances and trade-offs inherent in each one, we recommend reading *The CEO Tightrope*. The following chapters summarize each one—with a focus on actionable steps you can take to get your operating system up and running.

OWN THE VISION

W hat does it mean for a CEO to "own the vision" of an organization? It means that he or she takes responsibility for the overall vision of the group, including the strategy, mission, and values that guide it. This is the first responsibility of the CEO, because everything else that happens in the organization is—or should be—downstream of the vision. You have to know where you are headed before building and leading a team to get you there.

We use the word *own* because it implies a personal relationship between the CEO and the vision. To be an effective CEO, you must fully embrace the vision and feel it deep within your bones. The word *own* does not mean you personally created the vision. It may have been developed in a joint effort or been in place before you took over as CEO. Either way, it's your responsibility to understand and internalize the vision so deeply that it guides all your actions. You should be able to compellingly explain it to every stakeholder, from the most junior person to a highly sophisticated analyst to your average customer.

The overall vision you own is best expressed through three tools: a vision statement, a mission statement, and a set of differentiating values. This structure helps you convey the key facets of the vision to all your stakeholders, including the three constituencies we discussed in Part I: your employees, your customers, and your shareholders.

The **vision statement** expresses the idealized state your organization will create if it achieves its mission. It should be both aspirational and inspirational, as well as easy to remember. Consider for example Habitat for Humanity's vision statement: "A world where everyone has a decent place to live." In a few simple, memorable words, this statement describes what the world will look like if the team executes its mission. Key questions to consider as you craft or edit your vision statement include "What role in the world do we want this organization to play?" and "How will people live differently if our organization is successful?"

The **mission statement** is an expression of the mission itself. Key questions to consider here include "Why do we come to work every day?" "What makes us different from everyone else?" and "What is the essence of what we're trying to achieve?" Like the vision statement, the mission statement should be compelling and easy to restate. It should be something that helps any stakeholder quickly identify with the organization and see exactly why it needs to exists. For example, Hyatt's mission statement is "To provide authentic hospitality by making a difference in the lives of the people we touch every day." It takes the focus off the actual lodging the company provides and explains that its real mission is to foster a sense of hospitality and care at the individual level. That's something most people

USE STORYTELLING TO BRING THE VISION TO LIFE

Storytelling is a powerful way to bring the vision to life and help people remember it. The "Vision Story" is one tool Paul Smith recommends leaders use in his book *The 10 Stories Great Leaders Tell*. Smith encourages leaders to construct a narrative about the "picture of the future I'd like to help you create," including vivid details and characters showing what that changed world is like. Each of Smith's ten stories is a great tool for the CEO, but the Vision Story in particular helps people internalize the essence of what the company hopes to achieve. What is your Vision Story? Try writing it down or talking it through to a voice recorder.

can understand and appreciate quickly and gives the company a chance to set itself apart.

There's no rule that you have to have separate mission and vision statements worded just so. It's perfectly fine to combine them in one statement, as long as you're able to state compellingly why the organization exists and how the world will have changed for the better because it does.

The third piece of the structure is the set of **differentiating values**. Values add meat to the bones of the vision and mission statement and help shape the culture of the organization. And they help you and your team make better decisions. A good set of values must demonstrate the relative importance of some values over other values. This is in contrast to the many organizations who say their values are things like *honesty, integrity*, and *quality*—all things we expect in every organization, not something that sets you apart from others in your industry. Each value you establish should show a conscious trade-off the organization is making, thereby helping employees make better decisions on behalf of the company.

About fifty years ago, Southwest Airlines decided that "fun" was a value for that organization, and that the company would hire flight attendants based on personality versus traditional characteristics then thought to be suitable for flight attendants. Other airlines may value punctuality or low cost, but Southwest values fun and personability first, which helps them make different decisions. You can still see the results of Southwest's value differentiation today in their culture every time you step on one of their planes.

Values are only effective if they accurately represent what the executive team and CEO enforce. It does no good to come up with a great set of values and then allow yourself or your team to act in a way contrary to those values. It causes great damage when a team is led by an executive who clearly doesn't represent the values of the organization but is allowed to remain in place because they hit the numbers or deliver otherwise good performance. Once you've decided on the values, they must be adhered to by the CEO and executive team. If you want to change the values, that's fine, but as long as the values are what they are, supporting those fully is vital to building a good culture in the organization. We will discuss values at greater length when we get to the third responsibility, Build the Culture.

BALANCING ACROSS THE CONSTITUENCIES

As mentioned previously, your vision, mission, and differentiating values need to help each of the three core constituencies identify with the organization. For example, looking at the vision statement, employees, customers, and shareholders all need to be able to see "What's in it for me?" if the vision is achieved. Unfortunately, many companies become unbalanced by focusing on one of these groups to the exclusion of others. A classic mistake is the CEO focusing on shareholders to the exclusion of all others in their presentation of the vision. It's one thing to get shareholders revved up about all the money to be made, but your vision needs to bring along the employees who will put in the work and the customers who are going to hand over that money too. Furthermore, a skilled CEO can instantly tailor the vision in conversing with any of these groups, not at all changing it but presenting it in the manner that speaks most effectively to that group.

At NetQoS, where I first really cut my teeth as CEO of an enterprise, we were careful to set core values that represented ideas important to each of the three constituencies. For example, three of them were:

- We attract, cultivate, and retain exceptional talent well (employee focused)

- We're easy to do business with (customer focused)

- We're a profitable, growing company with long-term emphasis (shareholder focused)

What if you're a company that really does hope to differentiate in your area by being customer-first? That can work, but it should be stated and rewarded in a way that also brings in share-holders and employees. You'll need to explain to shareholders how customer-centricity represents a path toward creating long-term value, and you'll need to reward employees based on their own ability to serve customers outstandingly. If, conversely, you tell employees that the first value is delighting customers but then you give them a bonus structure around company profits, you have a misalignment not only between the constituencies but also between what you say and what you do.

INSPIRING BUT REALISTIC

One of the CEO's biggest challenges in owning the vision is doing so in a way that maintains your credibility. CEOs can sometimes become understandably excited about the vision of their company, but then get carried away to the point of making unrealistic claims about the future. If you're running around talking about how you're going to grow to some gigantic head-count in so many months, or hit such-and-such aspirational revenue goal by such-and-such time, you're setting yourself up for a big credibility gap down the road that will hurt your ability to lead as CEO. Try not to be the football coach who talks about the Super Bowl like a certainty in the first game of the season, spinning fantastic yarns about what might happen in the future. Instead, let your vision paint an inspiring picture of the destination without committing yourself to outlandish outcomes that aren't in your control.

It's tempting to step into the role of full-time cheerleader, but that's just one aspect of the CEO's role as owner of the vision. The balance you must seek is between galvanizing concerted action through excitement about the future, even as you give people a realistic assessment of what's possible.

The vision you own is the foundation of everything your company does. It should be deeply ingrained into its DNA, and present in some form in every meeting you hold, decision you make, and address you give.

It's hard to overstate the benefits when the CEO successfully owns a compelling vision. It brings together your existing team, attracts new talent, draws in customers, heartens shareholders, and imbues your whole team with a sense of shared purpose. Later in this section, we'll give you a tool for easily sharing the vision as part of your 1-Page Strategic Plan.

OWN THE VISION: BUILD YOUR PLAYBOOK

- **Create or review your company's mission and vision statements.** Make them brief and easy to remember.

- **Create or review your company values.** Follow the guidelines in this chapter to ensure the values are differentiating.

- **Create your Vision Story**, and consider using Paul Smith's book to write the other nine stories he recommends.

RESPONSIBILITY 2

PROVIDE THE RESOURCES

Your second responsibility as CEO is to provide your organization with the resources it needs to realize the vision. These resources come in two primary forms: *people* and *capital*. Often the second part of that equation—raising funds, ensuring profitability, overseeing cash flow, etc.—captures more of the CEO's attention. But as we saw in Part I, the people side demands just as much, if not more, of the CEO.

Once any company has achieved product-market fit and established itself as a viable business, its ongoing success hinges less on a specific product and more on the people it is able to attract, engage, and retain. The actual talent doing the work and the managers who oversee them define the future of the company. This is why, no matter the size or industry of the organization, the CEO must remain deeply involved in providing the resource of people.

PROVIDING RESOURCES: PEOPLE

The recruiting function of a company is not something the CEO should hand off to the HR department or a third party. Yet this is exactly what many CEOs do, especially in large companies. We think this is misguided: The CEO's time is always well spent on helping source talent and on ensuring that their own standards are met in recruiting at all levels of the organization. Getting the right people on the bus really is that critical.

It's common for companies to do more *hiring* than *recruiting*. By this we mean that they reactively look to hire talent once a position becomes available rather than continuously and proactively seeking out people who will be assets to the company. There is a massive difference between these orientations. **The company that only hires reactively misses out on top talent most of the time, because top talent usually isn't on the market exactly when you have an opening.** And they almost certainly aren't looking for opportunities on the job boards where your HR team posted the job. Rather, they are talking to their network and being approached by others. As CEO, you must lead the charge to find those people and be the ones they are talking to—whether or not you happen to have a suitable open position at this moment in time. For an exceptionally talented person, you may even want to create a position just for them. If they are really talented, they will create more than enough value to justify the expense.

If your company is only hiring a handful of people per year, the CEO should certainly be involved in recruiting and interviewing each of those people. Recruiting is a dual-sales process: the candidate needs to sell you on their capabilities at the same time that you need to sell them on the opportunity your company provides. Your direct involvement, along with ensuring that only great people are involved in the recruiting function at every step, goes a long way toward convincing high-value candidates to come on board. If the people they talk to in the interview process aren't top notch, the candidate will assume the rest of the company isn't top notch either.

Once you're hiring more than one hundred people per year, you may not be able to interview every serious candidate, though you should still be signing off directly on everyone hired in the top four or five layers of the organization. We strongly believe that you should still have one person in the organization who sets and maintains a high bar for those coming on board. Once you've scaled enough that it can't be you, consciously designate someone to perform this duty—it can often be an exceptional leader in the human resources or people department. Their goal is to enforce that consistent high standard across all departments and in all layers of the company.

The faster your business grows, the more you are in the people business. If you're growing at double-digit rates, you will need to hire a significant percentage of the total workforce every year. A 10 percent annual turnover rate coupled with a growth rate of 20, 30, or 40 percent means you will be hiring a significant percentage of your headcount in a given year. In our experience, many CEOs don't spend enough time ensuring they have built a productive machine for acquiring and engaging talent. But this segment of the organization is as vital as any other, if not more so.

Where exactly should you find these great candidates? You

and your organization need to put as much effort into that activity as you put into the activity of finding customers. This is always a vital task in a knowledge economy, but never more so than in recent years, when the United States has seen major labor shortages that cause many businesses to operate way below maximum productivity. You will be contending against direct competitors and even other industries for the same pool of top talent. It's worth spending time thinking about where you might find people who identify with your mission and vision, beyond a basic post on a recruiting website. These posts are unlikely to drive an influx of talent unless your employer brand is already highly valued in the market (i.e., if you're an Apple or a Tesla)—and even then, relying solely on job ads yields spotty results.

The first thing we recommend CEOs do is to **have conversations with their network to learn about the A-players they know, including those who might be open to making a job move soon.** This includes anyone in your life who you trust, from mentors to former colleagues to friends and family. Be known as the person who will always take a meeting with a talented person. Maybe it doesn't lead to anything immediate, but having these people on your radar is a huge asset. In addition, if you've done a good job hiring to start with, one of the best sources of such referrals is your own workforce, especially your A-players. Put together a program that makes it easy for employees to refer people they have worked with and can vouch for. This is an easy shortcut that can save your organization a lot of time, effort, and recruitment dollars.

Networking with other executives and university contacts is also an effective approach to recruiting. For example, I participated in the Austin Technology Council and made it a point to know at least the majority of the other CEOs around town so if a particular need for talent came up, I felt comfortable giving them a call, and they often did the same with me. These relationships also help validate employees you're seeking to hire. If I receive a call from a CEO recommending a particular employee, that person immediately moves to the top of my queue—as long as I view that CEO as credible.

Also **consider unique sources of talent you may be able to tap into,** places your competitors aren't necessarily looking. For example, I spent four years as an officer in the United States Navy and therefore knew how to read a military fitness report, the annual military performance review of its officers. In every fitness report or fitrep, they rank all the officers in a given year of a given command from top to bottom on their fulfillment of responsibilities, their character, their leadership, and more. If you have one hundred officers at a command, someone rated 30 on a fitrep would be in the top third of the command, a 24 would be in the top quarter, and an 8 would be among the top ten. That kind of real-world knowledge is hard to obtain in the civilian world, and is hugely valuable in seeking out quality employees. I knew that many of these strengths in the military would map well to certain jobs in the organizations I have led, and looking at the fitreps gave me an advantage in finding great people who wouldn't have ended up on our competitors' radars.

Similarly, **new graduates from colleges and universities that are a little out of the mainstream can offer an excellent pipeline of talent.** Seek out local colleges and try building relationships with their recruiting offices and, even better, key professors. These professors often have highly valuable perspective on top graduates with certain specialized or technical skills. Early in my CEO career, we pulled a great deal of talent from the engineering department at Louisiana Tech. My dad had been a university professor, so I knew all the professors there. They helped identify top graduates, and from there it was a pretty easy pitch to convince them to come work for a software company in Austin (most of the other recruiters approaching the school were from local power plants and paper mills). We had our pick of the litter thanks to a strategy our competitors took a good while to replicate.

You can also **look for disruptive events in the talent market.** Often these come in the form of events at other companies: layoffs, public relations challenges, drops in stock price, the departure of a key executive or the CEO. Anything that causes a shock within an organization often causes talent to become more receptive to working somewhere else. As part of the recruiting process, you must identify the companies you compete with for talent and continuously monitor them for the kind of disruptive events that make people look around for other options. Note that the companies you compete with for talent aren't necessarily the ones you compete with in the marketplace. From a recruiting perspective, your rivals are likely spread across geographies and industries. It can be hugely valuable to build relationships with executives at companies who have employees you want to hire. Several times, I've had discussions with CEOs who told me that, due to unfortunate circumstances, they were having to shut their business down and wanted to give me the first shot at hiring their top performers.

At other times, disruptive events in the talent market are the type that affect everyone, such as a recession. COVID-19 caused one of the greatest talent disruptions ever, leading to the "Great Resignation" that began in 2021. Some CEOs watched the intensified competition for talent and prioritized making

PARTING ON GOOD TERMS

One of the biggest gut punches a CEO can get is news that a great employee is leaving. How you handle this moment has lasting effects. Some CEOs resent the departing employee; they will ignore them for their last two weeks and feel stabbed in the back that the person is moving on. We feel this is short-sighted, because if they are A-players we want them to have the option to come back, and it's unfair because you should want what is best for them, even if that is an opportunity elsewhere. It may feel like a slight, but the CEO should congratulate the employee and recognize their contributions. This is not only the fair thing to do, but it will likely help you in your recruiting efforts down the road. Talented people who are thinking of joining your company often talk to former employees to hear about their experience. Your former superstars can also be excellent referrers of talent long after they leave. And if they have left on good terms, they may even be interested in coming back to the organization in a different role later.

I have even had situations where I talk with A-players in my organization and let them know that they are ready for the next step in their career, but that it may not necessarily be with this company. I am not telling them I want them to leave, but I am offering to help them make their next step by making connections or giving them a reference if our organization cannot provide the growth opportunity they seek. Some CEOs would panic at this prospect, but I have often found that having that conversation actually results in the person staying longer than they otherwise may have and being more selective about their next step rather than jumping at the first opportunity. And once they do leave, they feel supported and are very likely to talk to the A-players in their own network about their good experience at the organization.

their companies attractive to top performers who had left previous roles—and who often had a new set of priorities, such as
working remotely.

Common Recruiting Mistakes

Even though the recruiting process is critical to a company's survival—talent being the air your business breathes—companies
regularly make the same few mistakes in this area.

Mistake one is probably the most pervasive, and something
we alluded to previously: using a hiring process that only works
reactively and operates based on what's easiest for the company,
not what it takes to draw in superstars. For example, if the only
way to apply for a job at your company is by responding to a specific opening published on the company's website, you'll only be
able to hire on the company's timeline—which is likely not the
same timeline as the person who can make the most difference
in that role. Most A-players are rarely available, and you need to
work on their timeline. You'll have to grow your ability to find
them and scoop them up when they are ready to make a move.
This takes more effort and requires you to give people the ability to submit resumes to your organization without a position
clearly identified.

You may occasionally have a true superstar reach out using
such a mechanism. You and your recruiting team will then need
to further look into them, interview them in depth, and consider
where in the organization they might fit in. If you truly feel this
person is a superstar, you may create a position for them. Too
many organizations pass on A-level talent purely because there
is not a budgeted open role for them. But if your organization
is of any real size, a few additional people on the payroll won't

break the bank, especially if you are correct and the person is a real talent. In that case, they will create more value than they cost anyway. In other cases, you may need to cut loose low performers to make room for the superstars, though this isn't always strictly necessary. It's usually a matter of spending a little bit more money earlier than you thought, which often saves money down the road should someone else quit. If that happens, you now have a high-level employee in place to keep things going.

Applying this philosophy can be a little harder for smaller companies. If you have one hundred or fewer employees, you may only have a shot at bringing on a superstar here and there. Yet it is still worth doing, even when you are creating a position for them, because these people give the business a competitive advantage. Think of these hires as mini acquisitions. If one of your competitors went on the market at the right price and could add value to your business, you would try to buy them. It's the same with people. When they become available and will provide more value than they cost, you should be willing to hire them. This type of decision is well within your discretion as CEO.

The second common recruiting mistake is slow turnaround time. Candidates are most excited about a job the moment they submit their resume. If they hear nothing from you for days, weeks, or even months, their enthusiasm declines. They think, *Why doesn't this company recognize a great talent?* When you finally contact them, they're no longer enthusiastic. In the companies I have led as CEO, I always set an ideal two-week timeline from a top performer's submission of a resume to an offer being made. That means we had to move quickly on our process: a quick pre-interview with the chief recruiter; further interviews with four to six people from the company, including me, the chief bar-setter; interview debriefs; background and reference checks; and the final decision. But the speed allowed us to hire candidates who were also talking to larger companies that moved too slowly. We met the two-week deadline about 95 percent of the time. To make this process easier on your organization, never post a specific job that you're not ready to hire right now.

The third common mistake is thinking you're done once the offer is accepted. The process of providing talent spans the whole of the employment life cycle, including the absolutely critical phase of onboarding. Good onboarding immediately following the recruiting process is how you cultivate and retain exceptional people. Otherwise, you may end up going through a lot of effort to hire great people but then lose them quickly because of bad early experiences at the company. The new employee's impression of your organization will be formed in their first thirty days, and that impression will last a long time. A robust onboarding program is also a requirement for every person you hire, no matter how junior or senior that person might be. The onboarding function can be run by the same person who leads the recruiting function if the organization is on the smaller side.

Good onboarding starts with ensuring that everything the employee needs to do their job is ready the moment they walk in on their first day. We've seen companies where employees sit around twiddling their thumbs for a week before they get the basic technology and systems access they need to get started. Next, the onboarding facilitator should set up meetings between the new employee and everyone they need to know within the organization. It's good practice to have the employee meet with their boss on the first day (believe it or not, this doesn't happen in all companies) and go to lunch with their direct team in the first few days. This small gesture is an important step in integrating the new employee into the culture, building camaraderie, and helping them feel welcome. We also recommend setting up half-hour meetings where the new employee can meet all company executives, individually or in groups, within the first thirty days. In these meetings, executives should share prepared material on the role of their department, its key metrics, and how it supports the company strategy. This helps the new hire grasp how the company works together across its functions and sets the stage for positive working relationships.

It can also be useful to pair the new employee with a peer mentor, someone who has considerable experience at the organization and who can be the designated person to whom the new recruit brings questions. Anyone chosen as a peer mentor should be someone willing to shepherd their new peer and ensure they have a great onboarding experience.

Finally, recognize that the onboarding process lasts up to ninety days. It typically takes that long for any new employee to get fully up to speed and start delivering real value in their role. If you plunk the person down, don't help them orient, and don't give them proper coaching in how they are expected to contribute, you will start the relationship on the wrong foot— leading to frustration and potential micromanagement down the road.

Good managers at all levels are your biggest asset in ensuring great onboarding. Work with your human resources leaders to document the onboarding process as well as other aspects of the people-management process. This creates confidence and clarity for your managers and ensures that employees across the company are given a consistent employee experience. You can read much more about implementing a strong management system in my previous book, *The Manager's Playbook*.

CAPITAL: GROWTH VS. PROFITABILITY

In addition to providing the resource of talent, the CEO must also ensure that the company is well-funded and capitalized. Discussions of capital can become very technical very quickly, and it's difficult to offer CEOs general advice that applies across business types and situations. However, as part of this operating system, we can offer several principles to keep in mind as you provide your organization with financial resources.

The **first principle** is the need to recognize the continual trade-offs you must make between growth and profitability. Every CEO would like both, but in practice this is something like trying to turn left and right at the same time. High growth is almost always a drag on profitability, and vice versa. As CEO, you must decide which to prioritize at the current phase of the business. When you start out, growth is easy because you're beginning at $0. And if growth is high, you can drive valuation without turning a profit at all. There are many well-known examples of this: It took Amazon, founded in 1995, until 2001 to turn its first profit. Uber has yet to get there. But at some point, the business should become profitable, and the CEO may decide to shift away from growth goals and toward profitability goals. It's most important that the business first achieve positive *unit* profitability—the revenue associated with a unit sale minus the costs associated with selling that unit. Eventually, this should be followed by positive net income, which measures profitability including all expenses.

In balancing growth and profitability, consider the Rule of 45, which states that for a company to achieve a great valuation, its annual growth rate plus its operating margin should exceed 45 percent. This means that if you grow at a rate upward of 45 percent, you can break even or operate at a loss and still be rewarded in the market. Fast-growing companies often go through an IPO when they are still losing money because their growth rate is strong enough for people to believe in their ability to generate future profits. On the other end of the spectrum, if a company is not growing or is growing slowly, it needs an operating margin upward of 45 percent to achieve a high valuation. Use the Rule of 45 as a simple way to benchmark your business against the best.

The **second principle** is to prioritize the forecasting process. At its most basic level, this entails keeping a close eye on cash assets and ensuring they don't run out. This is the number-one reason startups fail, and it can of course also happen to established businesses as well. Unfortunately, we find that many organizations have no process for reliably predicting cash. Most accountants aren't trained directly on cash management, focusing instead on the P&L and backing into cash flow statements by removing the non-cash items. This is not particularly helpful for an operator who needs to understand where their cash goes and, importantly, the timing of when cash enters and leaves the business. Every CEO should have a strong understanding of how cash flows through their business and have a model that projects cash flow at least six months into the future; this model should be constantly refined and honed for accuracy. Available cash gives you options. Lack of cash reduces options and can easily cause a business failure. We encourage you to train your sales group to accurately predict revenue quarter by quarter. If they can forecast accurately how much they will bring in, you can in turn adjust resources to maximize growth without running out of cash.

The **third principle** to keep in mind around capital resources is the need for a balanced approach to spending and budgeting. Some CEOs tend to be tyrants around the budget. They instantly turn down any expense not accounted for in a rather tight budget, which can result in the business missing the boat on crucial opportunities as they crop up. On the other extreme, some CEOs are happy to blow the budget on new, exciting projects, even when their hopes are based on a sort of blind optimism. That approach can seriously eat into profitability as the business hemorrhages money. There's no easy way to strike the balance between some level of budget discipline and a willingness to make opportunistic investments in the future, but it's a tension that should continually be front of mind for the CEO.

One good practice is to ask yourself and your executives the two following questions: "What would you do if you had significantly more money to spend?" and "What would you do if you had significantly less money to spend?" These two questions force you and your executives to consider the cost/benefit trade-offs necessary to adapt to an ever-changing business climate. I've seen executives suddenly receive a windfall and spend it poorly because they had no plan. I've also seen executives forced to get by on significantly less, yet deliver close to the same productivity. Doing the thought exercise regularly about bigger or smaller budgets gets people thinking strategically and proactively about the decisions they make day to day.

▲ ▲

Beyond people and capital, there are other intangible resources you can offer as CEO. One is your reputation. Another might be some kind of special expertise you bring to the organization that it lacked before—especially if the organization was very inwardly focused and set in its ways. You might also bring in an advisor to help with areas where your current executive leadership team lacks skills. Ultimately, though, your primary responsibility in this area is to provide the organization with its two most funda- mental sources of fuel: the money it takes to make more money, and the people who make it all possible.

PROVIDE THE RESOURCES: BUILD YOUR PLAYBOOK

- **Write down what you feel your top sources of talent are.** What other unique sources can you cultivate? Who in your network can you connect with and have them refer talent to you?

- **Identify whether growth or profitability is your top priority right now.** What trade-off does this require?

- **Discuss the forecasting process with your executive team.** Work with your CFO on a continuous process for projecting cash flow at least six months into the future. Work with your head of sales on projecting revenue each quarter.

RESPONSIBILITY 3

BUILD THE CULTURE

Many CEOs talk about their business as a family. I've always felt that this was a poor mental model for understanding a business. The most glaring difference between a business and a family is the criteria for membership. In a family, you are stuck with the people you're related to. The task of family membership is to love and accept those people regardless of their abilities, interests, and flaws. You cannot choose who they are or jettison them when they don't create value for the family.

A business is quite different. Leaders must very explicitly choose who becomes part of the business, as discussed in the previous chapter. There are certain people in my family who I would be happy to work with, while there are others I would never employ. It's also the leader's responsibility to remove people from the business when their abilities do not align with the needs of the role available to them—something you can't do in a family.

The reason so many leaders nevertheless use the family metaphor for their business is because they want to convey the strength of the internal culture. They want to show that, as in a family, members of the organization feel deeply connected to one another, have each other's backs, and see each other as more than tools to be used. These are admirable traits in a culture. And it is indeed incumbent on the CEO to build up the culture of the organization; in fact, it is the third of the chief executive's five key responsibilities.

But when it comes to business, community is a better metaphor than family. We can think of a business as a *community of people who freely joined the organization because they agree on the mission, vision, and values of the organization.* This definition helps you think about the positive aspects of culture and belonging without the flawed comparison to relatives. As CEO, you fulfill a mayoral role in the community, and occasionally a chief of police role when crises arise. As the head of the community, you should not expect loyalty to you personally, as you might in a family context, but you can expect loyalty to the organization. CEOs who demand personal loyalty may be more likely to use the family metaphor, and they can fall into the trap of rewarding employees who avoid telling them the truth. As CEO, one thing you do *not* want included in your culture is encouragement of sycophancy at the expense of independent thinking and expression. Again the community comparison is more fitting. Members should be committed to the success and thriving of the larger group, but they need not be personally devoted to the leader. A leader who demands that type of devotion is often perceived by most as insecure.

There are also times when it makes sense for a person to leave a community. It may be because they are not meeting their obligations to the community, or because the community cannot provide opportunities for the growth and advancement the person desires. The role of CEO is to make the community the best it can possibly be so that great people want to be part of it for as long as possible, though there usually comes a time when even great people will be called elsewhere.

Over time, any community will naturally develop a culture: a shared set of values, attitudes, and behaviors. You may have heard the popular informal definition of culture: "how we do things around here." This collective ethos will develop whether it is intentionally built or not. As the head of your community, though, it's up to you to guide and shape the culture so it reinforces the behaviors you want.

WHERE DOES CULTURE COME FROM?

At the early stages of an organization, the culture will reflect the values and norms of the founder or founders. Because the team can all fit in one room and the founder is involved in most aspects of the business, the culture is built largely through who is selected to join the organization and what behaviors they observe in the founder.

As the organization grows, culture building requires more intention. Once you pass the mark of about twenty-five employees, and especially if you have people working in different offices or from home, the culture can easily become fragmented and chaotic. One team may have a very positive culture, while another's could become toxic. Interactions between different parts of the organization tend to decrease, causing silos with their own distinct and perhaps competing cultures. For example, the sales group may grow to think it is the most important sector of the organization, because the salespeople mainly talk to each other, look at their own data, and use their own systems. When groups are sealed off like this, cultural variations can develop due to the leadership style of a particular executive, the nature of the work or industry, or any number of hard-to-quantify factors in the chemistry of the people who make up the team. The purpose of a company culture is in part to grow shared values across these silos. It not only helps people feel like they are part of a larger team but also vastly increases coordination and collaboration.

The best tool for building a consistent culture past the startup phase is a strong set of values like those we discussed in Own the Vision (Responsibility 1). If you are a non-founder CEO and the founder is still an active part of the organization, it may be too early to capture new values, alter existing values, or have explicit conversations about the culture. If employees are still observing the founder regularly and taking cultural cues from them, your efforts to make these shifts could be confusing. But barring that circumstance, it is almost always an appropriate time to communicate about company values and culture. Start with your clearly stated, differentiating values and then work them into your communication as often as possible. Spotlight instances where an employee acts in accordance with a company value. Explain major decisions in the context of the company's values.

Another influence on the culture of the company is your own personality as CEO and what you personally value. This often happens unconsciously. For example, when a CEO with a Dominance personality in DISC terms talks about or to their organization, they almost always focus on driving results. Tangible outcomes and achievements are fundamental to how they define success. This orientation of the CEO may then shape the culture. Executives may begin to speak in similar results-oriented terms, and employees get the message that the thing the organization values most is rapid execution. If the CEO has an Influence personality, they will naturally emphasize relationships within the organization and care most deeply about whether employees feel personally motivated. In fact, they may argue that if everyone is highly motivated, the results will take care of themselves. That orientation of the CEO, like any other, will reverberate throughout the organization.

As discussed in Part I, the CEO must be aware of such effects they have on the team and ensure that they are leading *everyone* effectively, not just people who have similar outlooks on the world. A Dominance CEO isn't just the CEO of their fellow Ds—they also lead the Is, the Ss, and the Cs. This doesn't mean that you have to become a Frankenstein monster of all personality types, only that you must consciously understand your inclinations, capitalize on the parts that are positive for overall culture, and rein in the parts that might be destructive to a diverse organization of people who don't share your personality. The classic D CEO can certainly lean into their competitive spirit and desire to win. They might, for example, make celebration of achievements a key part of the culture. But they should temper this with awareness that harping on executives to show instant results and forcing people to do things the CEO's way are potential negative cultural permutations that might result from a Dominance personality.

Publishing your User Manual to the whole company is a good way to communicate what you value in a positive way. Recall that this is a short document in which you spell out your own approach to leadership, focusing on what is unusual about you, and explicitly state what you expect and value from the people who work for you. As mentioned previously, we recommend creating one version for your executives, with information on how they can best be an executive leader at the company, and another version with just the information that applies to employees at all levels of the company. Sharing such a User Manual clarifies how your own personality characteristics align with the company's differentiating values and influence the overall culture. You will find that having this information captured and easily shared prevents a lot of guesswork and misunderstanding and helps new people assimilate into the shared culture that much faster.

CULTURE-DEFINING VALUES

Clearly, we cannot tell you the specific values you should incorporate into your company's culture. Company cultures are like personalities—there are countless types that are quite different from each other but that work in their specific situation. The ones you choose for your company will be unique to your operation.

However, it is important that you think closely about the culture your stated company values will create. Culture is hard to pin down; it's more of a feeling and ethos than a rulebook. The set of values we encouraged you to create in Own the Vision (Responsibility 1) is the closest you'll get to a stable articulation of the culture. As we mentioned in that earlier chapter, it's vital to ensure that these values balance the interests of your three major stakeholder groups: employees, customers, and shareholders. If your values are balanced across the needs of these three constituencies, you have laid the foundation for a balanced company culture—one that attracts and engages your workforce, makes people want to do business with you, and shows shareholders that the operation is being run efficiently and effectively. To give you an example, let's revisit in more detail how we balanced these needs in our seven differentiating values at NetQoS.

Our first value was employee-centric: *We attract, cultivate, and retain exceptional talent.* We placed this at the top of the list because we wanted a culture that enabled us to attract and retain the best possible employees. Returning to this North Star allowed us to purposefully build a culture that prioritized the interests of the A-players we wanted to attract and keep around. For example, when we made decisions, we focused on how our top performers would react, not on how the bottom performers would. We also knew our culture couldn't be one where C-players were kept around indefinitely. Why? Because toleration of low performance is a surefire way to frustrate and drive away your high performers.

Is *We attract, cultivate, and retain exceptional talent* a differentiating value, though? Wouldn't every organization say they try to do this? Not all. McDonald's, for instance, understands that they can't be picky about getting exceptional talent. They therefore develop systematic processes and training to drive consistent behavior across their entire organization—ensuring stable performance even when star performers are a rarity. Some organizations may need exceptional talent in certain areas but not across the whole organization. At NetQoS, we set out to put value-creating superstars in every position possible. Focusing our hiring and management process on that cultural value became crucial to the way we did business.

Our second value spoke to all three constituencies but perhaps most to shareholders: *We will all act as co-owners and hold ourselves accountable.* This value typically resonates most with people who have owned and run their own businesses. I wanted to be sure we were communicating objective reality and being clear about our current situation as a company, especially to the board and investors. Stating explicitly that we all were to act as co-owners contributed to a culture where we faced reality—and it held me to that high standard as well. When I walked into a board meeting in September of 2002, twelve months after 9/11, my recommendation was to take the remaining funds in the business and order a shutdown because I couldn't tell them when a customer was going to buy a product based on the current economic conditions. Fortunately, we had a board member who said he believed in the company and more importantly, had a checkbook. "If you need additional funds, let me know," he said. The level of transparency and accountability we showed the board in that situation goes a long way to assuring key constituencies that the CEO will give them the straight scoop on the business.

The third company value was primarily customer-centric: *We underpromise and overdeliver.* I had dealt with many vendors over my career who did the opposite, consistently promising too much and delivering too little. Especially in an environment in which you're doing business with other companies, promising to deliver more than you can is a good way to get your advocate in that business into trouble. Your advocate will look bad politically, appear incompetent, and lose their ability and desire to advocate for you. This value led to our being perceived by our customers as great and having the highest NPS scores in the industry.

Another customer-centric value we upheld was *We are easy to do business with.* NetQoS catered to large corporations who could work with anyone they wanted to, and we realized that choosing a small company was a risk that also needed to have benefits for them. We decided that one of those benefits would be making it very easy to work with us. This meant we were always accommodating and professional not just in the sales process but also in contracting, invoicing, support, and all the other ways the customer would engage with us.

Our next value was *We are accountable to each employee.* Again, that word *accountability*, which we define as a willingness to face objective reality. If our second value was largely about all employees being accountable to the interests of the business, this value stated that company leaders would always be accountable to employees. We made a point to share with them all relevant information about how the business was doing, both good and bad, and to share with employees how they themselves were doing within the organization, both good and bad. We saw it as an important value for employees to expect objective reality from their manager and the executive team.

We are industry-driving performance experts was our sixth value, and it focused on both employees and customers. It was intended to reinforce our tagline, "Network performance experts," and help us continually strive to be the leading professionals on network performance anywhere in the world. If a customer had a problem involving network performance, we wanted them to immediately know that NetQoS was the company to call. This value had implications across the organization in terms of who we hired, how we trained, and how we continuously improved to maintain our status as the preeminent experts in the industry.

NetQoS's final value was shareholder-focused: *We are a profitable, growing company with long-term emphasis.* The focus on the long term was something that I had observed missing in many startups. In the early stages of a new venture, the emphasis is typically on short-term tactics and day-to-day survival. But once you've reached the point of product-market fit, the focus must shift to making decisions that ensure the sustainability of the enterprise long into the future. As discussed in Provide Resources (Responsibility 2), it is very difficult to be profitable and grow at the same time, especially when you're growing rapidly. That's why you don't often see the words *profitable* and *growing* together in the startup lexicon. However, this value was backed up with a more specific strategy. I told people that we wanted to grow as fast as we could while still making a single dollar. In other words, growth was the priority, but only so far as the unit economics made sense. We tended to reinvest all our money in the business and we knew that at any time we could cut back on growth investment and be more profitable for the shareholders. While it's virtually impossible to prioritize growth and profitability at the same time, it certainly is possible to balance them smartly.

These seven values lasted unchanged during nine years of operation and saw us through to a very successful exit. I think their lasting power had to do largely with the fact that they balanced the needs of employees, customers, and shareholders effectively, and thus created a positive culture that appealed to everyone involved.

CULTURE AND EMPLOYEE ENGAGEMENT

How do you know if you are doing a good job building the culture of your organization? It's not the easiest thing to measure. The closest proxy we have found for determining the quality of the culture is employee engagement. If your culture is strong, your employees are very likely to be engaged, and the opposite is also true.

There are several tools available for measuring employee engagement, but we are particularly fond of Gallup's Q^{12} survey because of its simplicity and the ability to compare your results across your industry. The Q^{12} survey asks employees to anonymously answer twelve questions about their experience at the company. Their answers are then rolled up and presented to you, offering a good overview of where engagement—and thus your culture—stands. Though not a perfect measure of engagement, we've found that the Q^{12} is directionally correct in just about every instance. (The questions themselves are also a great primer on what people need and expect from their managers. In addition to administering the survey itself, you can distribute these questions to every manager within your company so they can self-check whether they are covering these bases.)

Like any survey you give to employees, don't conduct the Q^{12} unless you intend to act on the results, no matter how surprising the results or how much they indict you or the executive team. Nothing destroys employee engagement more than asking people to take a survey and then dismissing the results as inaccurate or irrelevant, or simply never talking about the results again. Too many times we've seen CEOs ignore the issues surfaced by a Q^{12} survey, which is basically like ignoring smoke that's billowing from the organization. Employee engagement problems don't just solve themselves, and they aren't just due to a few bad apples in the organization, as some CEOs would like to think. Engagement problems are due to the systematic failure of managers to be effective and due to the failure of the CEO to drive a positive culture throughout the team.

Fortunately, the questions in the Q^{12} are specific enough that if you do score low in an area, you can easily brainstorm solutions with your executive team. Do present the results of the survey broadly to the organization, along with the changes you plan to roll out to address areas of weakness and bolster strengths. Give employees the opportunity to suggest their own ideas. You don't need to implement each one, but you should take in and consider them seriously.

We recommend administering the Q^{12} survey every six months, first for a baseline and then to monitor changes and evaluate how your interventions are working. After a much larger firm acquired NetQoS, we got a great illustration of the accuracy of the Q^{12} in measuring engagement and overall culture. We had been conducting the survey every six months for years and had been closely monitoring the results and working to improve weak areas. The scores had been consistently positive, with little variation for the last two or three years. When the ownership transaction closed, the acquirer initially made very few changes in personnel. The vast majority of people were still working for the same boss doing the same thing six months after the transaction closed (although I was no longer CEO). The biggest difference was that they were now part of a much bigger entity with a less defined vision, mission, and values, and a very different culture. We expected the survey to move slightly after the acquisition, of course, but were shocked when the results came back. Employee engagement as measured by the Q^{12} survey had dropped between 30 and 40 percent across the board in just six months. That's the kind of huge fluctuation in engagement that culture can cause, and the reason why CEOs must take their responsibility for culture building seriously.

THE SCARF MODEL

Author Blair Warren once wrote, "People will do anything for those who encourage their dreams, justify their failures, allay their fears, confirm their suspicions, and help them throw rocks at their enemies." Longtime leaders will recognize the truth in this statement. The human brain, while very complex, still has basic emotional reactions fine-tuned over tens of thousands of years. In their capacity as builder of the culture, CEOs must understand these human reactions and how the culture of the organization might be triggering them—positively or negatively.

Neuroscience expert David Rock's SCARF model, as outlined in his book *Your Brain at Work*, offers an excellent way to think about how culture causes such human reactions. The fundamental idea is that the same brain networks that seek to maximize reward and minimize threat for primary survival needs are also used in any situation where people interact. This means that when employees are working, they will constantly evaluate their environment through this filter. If they encounter a reward response they will tend to engage in a particular stimulus; and if they experience a threat they will disengage. While there are times that we can rationally override these instincts, it takes great effort and creates significant stress.

Rock's SCARF model presents five types of experiences that tend to activate a reward or threat response in the work environment: **status, certainty, autonomy, relatedness, and fairness**. CEOs should remain vigilant of these factors within their own organizations and strive to shape a culture that, as much as possible, stimulates the reward response in employees, thereby prompting greater engagement and higher chances of team success. Let's look briefly at each of the factors in SCARF.

Status

Status is the first and potentially most significant of the five areas. Signals that respect the employee's status cause a reward response, while signals that diminish their status cause stress. In *The Status Syndrome,* Michael Marmot describes a comprehensive study of British governmental workers and the relationship of status to life expectancy. He found that employees gained significant life expectancy the higher they moved up in the hierarchy of the British civil service. This finding may appear to be illogical because higher-level positions would usually be more stressful. However, it turns out that heightened status actually reduces stress. In higher positions, fewer people have authority over you, and you have more control—or at least perceived control—over your destiny. As Marmot points out, status also confers social benefits, with the people around you tending to give you more respect when your status is high.

There are many elements of a company's culture that send status signals to employees. A simple one is whether they are deemed worthy of access to information about the business and its performance. We will talk later in the book about the importance of transparent communication from the CEO. When employees are kept in the loop, they feel like important members of the organization—which they are. Working conditions, which as you remember are an aggravator in the motivational model, are another signal of status. Are your frontline employees given comfortable work spaces? Do they have the proper equipment and supplies needed to do their job? Do they have to park at the far end of the parking lot while your executives claim the prime spaces near the building?

Certainty

Certainty is the next factor that influences the threat or reward response. The human brain craves certainty around key facets of survival. Knowing where your next meal is coming from is a huge stress reliever for humans, for example.

In the work environment, one way certainty manifests itself is how much knowledge the employee has about what is really going on in the organization and any major changes that may affect them personally. If you don't provide this information, employees will not only feel their status diminished; they will also feel a threat to the certainty that they will continue to have a job. In the absence of communication from leadership, they may even make up their own story about what is going on. For instance, if the CEO meets with a group of people and it's unclear why they are meeting, a rumor may take hold that the business is for sale. This creates uncertainty and thus diminishes employees' ability to engage. It is critical to be transparent about the key issues facing the organization and to give people as much warning as possible around reorgs, layoffs, mergers, acquisitions, and other disruptive events. Some CEOs try to create a false sense of certainty by privileging this information until the last possible moment, but this paradoxically only diminishes feelings of certainty in the long run. If they know you'll pull the rug out from under them at any moment, they will tend to be on edge permanently.

Employees also appreciate the certainty that comes from knowing how their performance will be evaluated. We will discuss this more in Deliver Performance (Responsibility 5), but the organization should have a consistent system for delivering feedback to the employee and letting them know where they stand. Of course you can never eliminate all uncertainty from work or life, but strive to build a culture that makes the employee feel they are standing on solid ground.

Autonomy

A sense of autonomy tends to cause a reward response, while a lack of autonomy tends to cause stress and disengagement. Remember how *responsibility* is a critical source of motivation in the model we discussed in Part I? This is a similar concept. When people have control over their part of the organization, they tend to be more satisfied and excited about the job.

How can your company's culture instill more of a sense of autonomy? It could be as simple as giving people a small stipend to decorate their office in the way they want. More significant sources of autonomy include allowing people to make decisions within their domain (more on that in the next chapter) and set their own goals for the quarter (more on that in Responsibility 5, Deliver Performance). Be on the lookout for other ways to give people a reasonable amount of input into their day-to-day work environment and a sense of self-determination within their role.

Relatedness

Most people want to feel like they are a part of the community they have chosen to join in taking their current job. Many companies that are renowned for their culture put a great deal of effort into social events for employees, precisely because these events create more relatedness and, in turn, more engagement. While such social events are typically a good idea in the context of any culture, they are not the only way to foster relatedness within the organization. For example, we talked in Part I about the value of personality assessments and User Manuals. When people share these with each other and get to talking about who they are as people, they begin to bond at a deeper level. You will likely have a few people who balk at personality assessments and who may disagree with their results. That itself is a great start to a conversation. They can talk with colleagues about why they feel that way and put it in their User Manual, and their employees will understand that facet of their personality.

Another tactic for creating relatedness in your culture is being intentional with onboarding, as discussed in the previous chapter. That first lunch out with the boss and new colleagues can set the stage for deeper relationships. And the chance to meet with each executive in the company over the first thirty days puts faces to names and makes it easier for the new employee to reach out as needed in the future.

Fairness

The final factor in David Rock's SCARF model is fairness. We develop our innate sense of fairness early in life, as anyone who has raised kids will tell you. In the work context, we tend to react negatively when we perceive that someone in the organization was treated unfairly, whether it was ourselves or a peer. This perception of fairness rests entirely in the eye of the employee. And if employees at large begin to perceive that the organization doesn't treat people fairly, you're going to have serious cultural issues.

Pay is of course one of the areas in which concerns around fairness arise. As discussed in Part I, we encourage CEOs to establish a pay policy in which people are paid close to market rates for their roles. Pay fairness really begins to aggravate people and cause cultural issues (a) when people are across the board paid below market rates, without some other clear compensation for this factor, as you might find in a passion-driven nonprofit; or (b) when some people are paid below-market rates for their position and experience while others are paid significantly more.

In the next chapter, we will also discuss process fairness—the practice of clearly communicating how leadership came to certain decisions. This ensures that even when employees don't like the decision you made, they at least understand the rationale behind it, which usually increases their perception of fairness.

We've seen that an organization is like a community—not a family—and that this community will naturally develop its own culture over time. Your third responsibility as CEO is to actively and intentionally shape this culture. The culture you build should be rooted in your company's differentiating values, and it should attract talent, make customers want to do business with you, and reassure shareholders that the organization is healthy.

BUILD THE CULTURE: BUILD YOUR PLAYBOOK

- **Use Gallup's Q^{12} survey to measure employee engagement.** Follow through immediately on findings. Plan to run the survey again every six months to keep a pulse on engagement levels, which are a good proxy for the health of your culture.

- **Consider how your culture affects each area of the SCARF model.** Are there changes you can make to ensure that these five factors provoke reward responses, rather than threat responses, in your employee base?

BUILD A DECISION-MAKING ORGANIZATION

Decisions are the fuel on which every organization runs. The success of your business hinges on how well decisions are made and communicated within it.

As CEO, you are the chief decision maker. When the organization is small, this is a tough but manageable responsibility. You can easily see the big picture and the details at the same time, and you can usually gather all the information you need to make a reasonably informed decision. If a decision turns out to be wrong, the smaller organization can usually pivot back pretty quickly.

But as the organization grows, especially past the fifty- to one-hundred-employee mark, decision making takes on greater complexity. You've got a lot more people to consult, many more factors going into the decision, tons more data, and a lot more riding on getting the decision correct. Many CEOs mistakenly try to cling to decision-making authority in this context. They feel it's their duty to make all the decisions, even the ones more appropriate for others in the company to make. They therefore become a decision bottleneck and slow the whole organization down.

We will talk in Part III about how CEOs can build their own decision making as a skill. But the broader topic we are concerned with in this chapter is your fourth responsibility as CEO: *to build a decision-making organization*. While you will always retain the job of making the big, irreversible decisions that affect the whole organization, you must empower everyone on your team to make smart, timely decisions within their own domain, only escalating decisions to superiors when the matter is truly beyond their authority.

Once the organization grows past that critical fifty- to one-hundred-person mark we keep mentioning, the CEO role fundamentally changes from sole decision maker to chief direction setter. At this point, **your ultimate goal is to empower employees to make the same decision that you would make as CEO if you were in their position**—i.e., if you had all the relevant information and expertise they have in their role. To do this, you need employees at all levels to combine their on-the-ground insight and domain expertise with the big picture of the company's mission, vision, values, strategic objectives, and near-term goals. Bridging that gap makes up a great deal of this fourth responsibility of the CEO.

ABOVE OR BELOW THE WATERLINE?

In an organization that makes decisions well, decision-making authority is properly distributed across the workforce. How is this done? You can start at the top by creating clarity around which decisions your executives are authorized to make on their own and which they should consult you on. This discretionary authority may be different for each executive based upon your comfort level with their judgment, the quality of their previous decisions, and their experience level. In the following chapter, we will create Executive Performance Profiles for each member of your leadership team, and this will include specifics around their authority. There are, however, general rules around when the executive should make the decision and when they should escalate to you for broader discussion.

A simple way to explain decision-making authority to executives is to draw a ship on a whiteboard and then add a waterline going through its middle. If the ship takes a hit above the waterline, it won't sink. But if the ship takes a hit below the waterline, there is a strong possibility that it will go under. Explain to your executives that their job is to make all the decisions in their area of responsibility that are above the waterline. They can, of course, consult with you as CEO, but if the decision is above the waterline, you are going to ultimately have them make the call. If, on the other hand, the decision is below the waterline—i.e., it could sink the ship—they need to have a discussion with you, the CEO.

Consider a sales executive who comes to you asking whether they can give a 10 percent discount to a customer. This relatively inconsequential discount is well above the waterline and thus within the sales executive's realm of authority. As CEO, you would tell them it's their decision to make. Don't let executives pass the buck on such decisions that are within their scope of authority.

But what if that same sales executive came to you with a decision to give a big customer a 90 percent discount and promise them five new features in the product by next quarter? In that case, the decision is below the waterline. It could turn this key customer relationship into an unprofitable one, and it also places a demand of new features on the product team, which is outside the sales executive's area of responsibility. Here we see another important principle of decision-making authority: If the decision laterally affects areas of the organization beyond the decision maker's domain, that decision should be escalated to the manager above for discussion. When decisions fall near the waterline or the potential lateral effects are debatable, have an open discussion with the executive about these complexities.

These conversations are important to training your executive team to make decisions that are good for the company, and as rapidly as possible, while still maintaining the integrity of the ship. These conversations should cascade down the organization, too, with each manager communicating to employees about what decisions are theirs to make and when to pass the issue upward. (Remember that responsibility is a big motivator, as discussed in Part I. Giving people full authority to make decisions in their domain is a great way to boost it.) The goal of this process is a network of decision makers, each making judgment calls as close to the heart of the issue as possible. Often decisions are best made by the frontline employee, at their workstation or in an impromptu conversation.

GUIDELINES FOR DECENTRALIZED DECISION MAKING

What other principles apply as you distribute decision-making authority across the organization? Here are a few you can instill from the top. Practice these in your own decision making, and help others do the same.

First, **encourage speed in decision making**. The value of a decision tends to decay as time passes. Deciding quickly and with conviction is not the same as deciding thoughtlessly. Instill in your executives and other employees the principle that faster decisions are generally better than getting caught in analysis paralysis. A lot of people, including CEOs, become paralyzed into inaction when faced with difficult decisions. They just can't force themselves to do something that causes significant pain or carries substantial risks. But it's important to understand for yourself—and communicate to other decision makers—that when you're not doing something, the world will not stop and wait for you.

It's also wise to **differentiate between reversible and irreversible decisions**. Most decisions are reversible and can be changed without too much impact on the organization. For reversible decisions, speed is of the essence. Should contrary facts become available or unintended consequences emerge, you need to consider the data and quickly change course as required. Other decisions are irreversible. These are the only decisions that should not be made quickly, especially when they are significant—things like making an acquisition or selling the company. This type of decision usually makes up 5 percent or less of the decisions you must make as CEO. They require longer discussions and thinking through the second- and third-order effects of each path forward.

In making decisions, also encourage people to **balance the needs of employees, customers, and shareholders**. As we have discussed, taking account of these sometimes competing interests is a big part of your job as CEO, but employees throughout the company can use this rubric as well. As they consider options, they can think through what the *customer* would want them to do, what their fellow *employees* would think best, and what the company's *shareholders* would encourage. The right decision usually lies at the middle of that Triangle of Tension.

Employees should also **consult the company mission, vision, values, and strategic objectives** when making decisions. Again, you want them to make a decision similar to the one you would; if they have internalized the big-picture direction of the company, they likely will. In the next chapter, we will create a 1-Page Strategic Plan that gives everyone easy access to this information in one place.

Consulting the org chart can also be helpful as employees make decisions. It helps reinforce the principle we discussed above: If the decision affects other groups laterally, they should escalate the decision. But if the effects will be felt primarily through their own chain of command, they have authority to make the decision on their own. We have found it helpful to make posters of these three things just mentioned—the Triangle of Tension between employees, customers, and shareholders; the 1-Page Strategic Plan; and the organizational chart—and place them around the office (or within digital tools) to aid people in making good decisions.

Next, **make your people take a position** when the decision authority belongs to them. If an executive wants to discuss an above-the-waterline decision with you, make them propose a carefully considered path forward. If you have hired well, they

THE STARTUP ADVANTAGE

CEOs of large companies often marvel at what tiny startups can achieve in a small amount of time—things that would take the large company many times as long. The primary reason for this is the speed of decision making at startups. While big companies often have advantages in terms of resources (more capital and more people), startups are a lot more agile. A startup can usually make five decisions in the time it takes a big company to schedule a meeting to make one decision. This means they can react super-fast to market changes, technology shifts, changing customer desires, and more. It's a constant series of pivots that startups can accomplish but large companies usually cannot. However, by decentralizing decision making and placing a premium on decision speed, even large companies can prevent bottlenecks and harness some of the startup's advantage.

will be smarter than you in their area of expertise. To make the best decision possible, meld your unique experience and big-picture vision with their knowledge of their area. They should do the same with the people who work for them.

Giving people authority to make decisions in their area means that **you should not overrule your people often**. If your team is applying the company's mission, vision, values, and strategic objectives when making decisions, they will probably come to a decision you agree with. However, if you often find yourself at odds with decisions your team is making, look for the underlying problem. Could you and the employee be misaligned on the big picture? Do you have different assumptions about what will create value? While achieving consensus is not always possible, frequently overruling your team is not desirable either. Balancing between these extremes is critical to success.

Finally, when someone makes a decision, **give them credit if things go well**. If it doesn't turn out to be the right decision, back them up and look for solutions. The thing *not* to do is to blame others when something goes wrong, or to appear to soak up credit for a smart decision made elsewhere in the organization.

DEPARTMENT VS. DEPARTMENT

CEOs are called upon to make decisions that span the various departments of the organization. Remember that each of these departments can be thought of as a point on the two Triangles of Tension: employees (HR), customers, and shareholders (finance); and sales, marketing, and product. Natural conflicts exist between these interests—between sales and marketing, marketing and product, employees and customers, and between finance and everybody else. You have the job of quickly and clearly refereeing disputes that arise among these groups. It's an aspect of the CEO job most people don't envy.

What's the best way to handle such conflicts? First, be sure you are spending your time impartially across all these functions of the organization. It's easy to play favorites. You may have a tendency to believe that one department is more critical than the others and thus spend a lot of time with that group. I've known CEOs who seemed to be attached at the hip to their CFO or another executive in their organization. Or, you may simply get along on a personal level with one or two executives in a way you don't with the others. Whatever the case, devote equal time to each executive leader within the organization. When conflicts arise, you will be better positioned to look at the issue fairly, and one side won't feel that the decision you make is based on personal connections or biases.

Second, **coach executives on bringing cross-departmental issues to you quickly,** rather than waiting because they believe they are supposed to solve it themselves. If they wait, the impasse will stand, the decision won't get made, and divisions may deepen. The earlier you are made aware of the conflict and can lead it toward a positive resolution, the better.

Third, **give up any aspiration you have to "lead by consensus."** Some CEOs are natural consensus builders, which can be a great asset, but they will struggle when their primary goal is for everyone to just get along. It's rare that any decision affecting multiple departments will please all the stakeholders, but you still need to make the decision. The fact that full agreement hasn't been reached should not be an excuse for putting off a decision that needs to be made. Rather than aiming for perfect consensus, make a decision that aligns with the mission, vision, values, and objectives, then ask those who disagree for their buy-in once you have explained your reasoning.

HOW SHOULD THE
BOARD CONTRIBUTE?

If you have a formal board, its members are a constituency who play a significant role in decision making. If you have public shareholders, the board theoretically represents the shareholders, though of course the board and the shareholders will not always agree. If your company is privately owned, the board's relationship is more directly with you as the CEO. In either case, the CEO must learn when to include the board in decision making and how to leverage their insight fully.

We generally advocate for an unintrusive board. This means the board is responsible for their usual duties—hiring and firing the CEO, evaluating the CEO's performance, and ensuring good governance and compliance with applicable laws, regulations, and ethical business practice—but has a narrow scope beyond that. The board should always be consulted on the company's strategic objectives and quarterly goals, which we will discuss in the next chapter, but they should usually not be involved in the day-to-day operation of the business.

Many CEOs get in trouble when they involve the board in decision making in a messy or unstructured manner. First, it's wise to set explicit parameters around decision-making authority, just as you do with your own executives. Agree on the following with the board: which decisions are yours to make without consulting the board (e.g., purchases within the budget up to $2 million); which decisions are yours to make after informing the board (e.g., replacing an executive); and which decisions you can make only with explicit board approval (e.g., an acquisition or divestiture).

Second, understand the difference between advice and instruction from the board. As an organization, the only way a board acts officially is by a vote, like Congress, and it almost always votes unanimously. However, there is often one board member who is outspoken and forceful with their opinions. CEOs often feel obligated to follow those opinions when in reality they should be regarded as one person's suggestions—not as instructions for what the CEO must do. As CEO, remember that board members don't think about your business every day. They may not even think about your business every month. With meetings scheduled once per quarter, they do not have sufficient information to form an opinion on most operational aspects of the organization—unlike you and your team. They may also come from an industry different from yours or be influenced by their own background in a specific functional area of business. Certainly, you must be prepared to suffer the consequences if you ignore a board member's advice and then perform poorly. But you should always be clear with the board that unless there's a board resolution passed by a vote, everything said by board members is a suggestion, not explicit directions.

Two good rules of thumb are to not ask the board's permission if you don't need it, and to not ask the board's advice if you don't want it. If you have already decided on one course of action, what happens when you take it to the board and one or two members push you to go a different direction? In this scenario, you have only raised a problem you didn't have before. Instead, use your board strategically. Where they can be of most help is in establishing the strategic objectives of the organization for the next two to three years and in setting appropriate quarterly goals at the company level (we will talk more about both of these in the next chapter). Ultimately, you as CEO own the process, but your board's insight can be valuable on these bigger strategic matters—more so than in tactical or operational matters. What's needed from the board is to hire a CEO with the right knowledge, skills, and experience (that's you), let that CEO do the job, and fire them if it doesn't work out.

THE FOCUSED BOARD MEETING

The CEO's relationship with the board has a dynamic unlike any other in the organization. They are technically the CEO's "boss," even though the CEO retains full responsibility for organizational outcomes. Plus, the CEO usually sees them only once a quarter and must manage their meetings. Here are further suggestions for running great board meetings each quarter.

First, prepare a board package and send it out at least forty-eight hours before the meeting. We recommend including the following:

- A **letter from the CEO**, in which you summarize the past quarter and share your thoughts about the company's current state and future. This is a good place to set the tone for the meeting. Allude to any strategic issues you would like to discuss in the meeting or any decisions you would like input on.

- An **organizational chart**, to reinforce structure and key people to the board.

- **Detailed bios of the board members**, highlighting each one's unique experience and knowledge. This not only helps the members of your board work better together; it is also a good reminder for you of the various talents that are part of your board's brain trust.

- The company's **1-Page Strategic Plan.** We will discuss this in the next chapter. This document contains the company's mission, vision, values, strategic objectives, and quarterly goals.

- **Outcomes of previous quarter's goals**, indicating whether or not each was achieved. Add any context you feel is relevant, whether it's celebrating a win or exploring the causes and implications of a miss.

- **Summarized departmental data.** Include any data from the various departments that pertains to top-level goals. Limit this to information that gives the board real insight. Include financial data, but understand that you do not need to go through the full P&L and balance sheet in the board meeting; this is not a good use of the board's time. Round out financial data with information about other key parts of the business, including employees and customers.

Put the board package in PDF format before sending. Your opening letter may go in the email to which you attach the PDF. Also, be sure to warn board members ahead of time about any unexpected news in the board package or the meeting itself. The best board meeting, for everyone involved, is one without surprises.

Now, what should happen in the board meeting itself? We recommend that you begin the meeting with an overview of the mission, vision, values, and strategic objectives. Has anything changed? What progress has been made in the big picture? Then you can move to the outcomes of the quarterly goals. How are things going in each of the six areas of the business? Resist the urge to go into cheerleader mode. Don't wriggle out of bad news or change metrics on the fly to make things look better. Yes, you want the board to be excited about the future of the company, but you also need to be candid about the current state. We have attended far too many board meetings that felt like the CEO was conducting an infomercial for the company. This reduces the board's trust in your ability to present them with objective reality.

From here, you may turn things over to each of your executives for a brief overview of their function. Instruct your executives to avoid data deep dives. Ideally, they will present one or two slides apiece, focusing on the outcome

(continued)

of their goals for the quarter and trends in their KPIs. The board should feel they are getting critical strategic take-aways from these short presentations, not drinking from a firehose of data.

In the last part of the meeting, discuss the proposed company goals for next quarter, ending by reviewing any outstanding decisions or other matters. The board will thank you if you are able to keep these meetings brisk and focused on items where they can add value. As we have mentioned, that is usually not in detailed operational discussions.

Finally, we recommend that CEOs directly ask board members for feedback. At your next board meeting, ask them to do a little homework. Have each member write down (a) three things you are doing well as CEO and (b) three things you could improve on as CEO, then follow up with them later to get their answers. Repeating this process a couple of times a year can significantly build up the CEO's self-awareness and align expectations between the board and the chief executive.

PROCESS FAIRNESS

A final concept to understand as you build a decision-making organization is *process fairness*. This term refers to employees' perception that decisions made within the organization are fair—that they are arrived at by careful, consistent thought rather than arbitrary or secretive agendas.

In an article in *Harvard Business Review* ("Why It's So Hard to Be Fair"), Joel Brockner of Columbia Business School describes the three drivers of process fairness: (1) whether employees had any say in the decisions that was made, (2) whether the decision was made based on consistent data and reasoning versus a biased perspective, and (3) how the decision makers communicate the decision and take in employee reactions. The CEO must consider these drivers, especially when making and communicating decisions that are likely to upset some portion of employees. Brockner shows that process fairness is often more important than the outcome itself; people can react positively to ostensibly negative outcomes when the process is perceived as fair. Layoffs are a classic example of where process fairness is required. You, as CEO, must explain to people why the cuts were necessary, how you decided who to lay off, and what it means for those who remain.

As soon as you make a decision that affects your workforce, sit down and write a couple of paragraphs in an email to the entire organization, communicating the decision and the reasons behind it. Reference the company's mission, vision, values, and strategic objectives, and any other factors that drove the decision-making process. This communication will enable everybody to walk in the next day knowing exactly what was decided and believing that the process was well-reasoned and fair. It matters less *what* the decision is and more *how* you contextualize and explain it.

BUILD A DECISION-MAKING ORGANIZATION: BUILD YOUR PLAYBOOK

- **Hold a meeting with your executives to discuss decisions that fall above and below the waterline.** Discuss examples of both types of decisions. Encourage executives to bring decisions that are below the waterline to you quickly. Ask them to do the same when decisions involve competing agendas across departments.

RESPONSIBILITY 5

DELIVER
PERFORMANCE

Almost all executives have mastered the basic skills of project management. Over their careers, they grow to understand concepts such as breaking large projects into tasks, assigning out the tasks, ensuring people complete them on schedule, and rallying everyone around the deliverable. This adds up to the ability to deliver tangible outcomes within a set budget and timeline—which is essentially the definition of a successful executive.

These executive-level project-management skills are highly valuable. But the CEO role calls for a very different approach. Why?

First, while the CEO operates within a budgetary framework, it is the CEO themselves who decide what the budget should be and what strategic priorities it should support.

Allocating capital is a very different skill from managing a fixed budget. Second, while the executive handles a relatively narrow functional area, the CEO must operate across all company functions, overseeing strategic activities that impact every part of the business. Finally, much more than other executives, the CEO must consider stakeholders outside the organization just as much as those inside. As we have discussed, they must be constantly aware of the needs of shareholders and customers as well as of employees, and balance the interests of those three groups effectively. For these reasons, a simple task-oriented approach to the CEO role is doomed to failure in the long term. Basic task management *can* temporarily work for a CEO with fewer than, say, twenty-five employees. But as the organization grows north of one hundred employees, the number of projects and tasks begins to increase exponentially. At several hundred employees, and certainly beyond that, complexity grows to the point that it is impossible for the CEO to track individual tasks. If the CEO doesn't recognize this shift and move beyond a task-oriented approach, they will find themselves working harder and harder but getting less and less done.

So, if task orientation isn't right for the CEO role, what is?

The answer lies in *enterprise* orientation. Enterprise orientation is different from task orientation in several key ways:

1. **Enterprise orientation sets the direction rather than following it.** Every other executive can look upward from their department for direction from the corporate level: What is the business trying to achieve? How does my group contribute? Not so for the CEO, who must instead establish this direction. This may seem obvious, but far too many CEOs fail by not articulating the basic

strategic objectives of the organization and communicating about them consistently. They seem to think the objectives are implicit, when in reality they are anything but. We will discuss a tool for clarifying strategic direction in this chapter.

2. **Enterprise orientation takes a systems view.** The CEO's job is to maintain a holistic view of the business and understand how its constituent parts contribute to the fundamentals of the business. Only from that vantage can you identify misalignments, facilitate cross-functional partnership, and reinforce the strategic objectives to everyone, adjusting the direction as needed.

    When the CEO falls back into task management, they have left enterprise mode and are no longer providing distinctive value to the organization. Yes, occasionally the CEO may be called upon to pinch-hit within a business function, such as helping to close a major sales deal, but the CEO's first job is to operate above and outside any particular function. As my friend Jim Schleckser notes in his book *Great CEOs Are Lazy*, the best CEOs don't spread their time equally around like peanut butter on a slice of bread. They instead allocate their time where it really matters. Ninety percent of the time, you have the most impact working on optimizing the system that is your business—not on managing individual projects.

3. **Enterprise orientation requires continuous forecasting.** CEOs have the difficult job of managing the future. Unless you have a crystal ball, this requires the CEO to continuously analyze diverse inputs and project what they mean for the future. What is happening in your industry? Where is technology headed? What

are competitors doing and saying? What are you hearing from your employees and customers? How is the business performing against its objectives? All of these and many more should shape your running vision of the future and what it means for your company. This is a longer-term and more robust vision of the future than is required to deliver a project on time. Rather than trying to produce quality on a deadline, you're steering a whole enterprise toward an unfamiliar horizon, which requires constant vigilance and forethought.

An enterprise mindset is required if you want to deliver earnings, growth, and other measures of top-level performance, which is what the board and shareholders will rate you on at the end of the day.

THE 1-PAGE STRATEGIC PLAN

The 1-Page Strategic Plan is a simple tool that helps you reinforce your own enterprise orientation and provide strategic clarity to the organization. In a single page, it links strategy to performance. Flip to p. 149 for a template.

At the top of the page goes the organization's **mission and vision statements**, as developed in Responsibility 1 (Own the Vision). These are true north for everyone in the company. All employees, including your frontline workers, should be able to state the mission and vision and contextualize it in their own words.

Next come your **differentiating values**, also developed in Responsibility 1. As we discussed, the values provide the foundation of your organizational culture and help people make strategically sound decisions in their day-to-day work. As with the mission and vision, your workforce should see the values often, hear about them from you and other managers, and know them by heart.

With this foundation paved, the 1-Page Strategic Plan now moves on to the company's **strategic objectives**. These are the performance benchmarks you hope to achieve looking out over a two- to three-year period. In writing them, you want to answer this question: *If we execute our strategy successfully, what tangible outcomes should we be able to attain in each functional area of the business?* Start the objective-setting process with the two Triangles of Tension:

- External tensions between shareholders, customers, and employees.

- Internal tensions between sales, marketing, and product.

In each of these six areas, write down *the* one or two critical things the organization needs to accomplish over the next two to three years. As you draft these strategic objectives, use the following guidelines:

- **Include a clear measurement for each objective.** There should be no ambiguity about whether the strategic objective was met or not met at the end of the two to three years.

- **Limit to one or two objectives per area.** This is not a glorified to-do list. It's a record of the top strategic priorities. (Remember, you are in enterprise mode, not task mode.) True priorities are inherently limited in number. Some objectives may cover overlapping areas—for example, a sales goal could also relate to shareholders.

- **Aim for a balance of challenging but realistic.** These are not pie-in-the-sky wishes but objectives you believe the organization can actually achieve if it aligns and focuses. Managing the future requires being able to project what the business will achieve with a baseline of confidence. If you're shooting for the moon in all six functional areas, performance will be unpredictable. And in the eyes of the board and shareholders, unpredictable performance is anathema.

Whether you are updating strategic objectives that already exist or writing them new, **include your executive team in the process**. Start by blocking out time on your calendar and devoting your full attention to what you think the strategic objectives should be. Then set up a meeting with your executive team to get their ideas. Hear all perspectives on what your internal leaders think is strategically critical in that two- to three-year time frame. Encourage constructive disagreement. Take good notes. Recognizing that full consensus will be impossible, it is then your task to take these perspectives and draft the final set of strategic objectives that go in the 1-Page Strategic Plan. It's also a good idea to bring your board in on this process. Once you have a strong idea of what you think the strategic objectives should be, you can initiate a discussion at the next board meeting to get their input.

The final portion of the 1-Page Strategic Plan further tightens the focus by clarifying the **quarterly company goals**. While strategic objectives for the next two to three years are critical, they alone are usually not sufficient to drive execution. For most organizations past the startup phase, goal setting at the quarterly level is most appropriate. We recommend quarterly goals rather than annual goals for a variety of reasons, including the seasonal nature of most businesses and the ability to make decisions on the most current information. This cadence allows you to align and realign the organization by quarter as the on-the-ground situation changes. Furthermore, quarterly goals allow the team to feel gratification when near-term milestones are achieved and to learn lessons when a goal is missed. The quarterly goals you establish at the company level will lay the foundation for similar goals set at the executive, middle, and frontline levels of the organization.

As you draft the quarterly goals:

- **Use your strategic objectives as the starting place.** Quarterly goals result from breaking down strategic objectives into pieces that can be achieved in the next ninety days. Ask, "What is the most important thing to achieve this quarter to get us closer to the objective?"

- **Ensure that everyone can contribute.** As with the strategic objectives, think through the six areas of the business and what goals may be appropriate in each area. If you only set sales or financial goals, other parts of the organization will feel left out of the plan, and you won't have clarified what success looks like for the group as a whole.

- **Choose relevant measurements.** Each goal should incorporate a measurement or proof point that specifies exactly how you will know the goal has been achieved. For example, you can measure sales goals many different ways: a dollar amount in bookings, growth in recurring revenue, conversion or win rates, accuracy of sales forecasts, etc. You will need to decide which measurements reflect the most value for your business right now.

- **Use SMART as a final check.** The classic SMART guideline is a good way to validate that you have written strong quarterly goals. Each goal should be Specific,

Measurable, Achievable, Relevant, and Time-Bound. (Because these are quarterly goals, they are inherently time-bound, though you may in some cases need to set a deadline that occurs before the end of the quarter.)

You can create the quarterly goals using a process similar to the one recommended for the longer-term strategic objectives. Two weeks before the start of the quarter, ensure that you've given thought to goals for the upcoming period, then meet with the executives to plan for the quarter. It is wise to distribute your draft goals to executives before the meeting to show the milestones you believe would show progression toward achievement of the strategic objectives and give each person a chance to think about the implications for their group. The first few of these quarterly planning meetings may be chaotic and take a while. But as you instill the discipline of quarterly goal setting, you can usually get this done in a thirty- to forty-five-minute meeting that gets everyone aligned for the upcoming cycle. You should also be presenting these goals to the board at the quarterly board meeting to ensure they understand priorities for the coming period.

Once you've got the quarterly company goals established, they should go in a fresh version of the 1-Page Strategic Plan that is sent to every employee. Now, in one place, **each person can see the mission and vision that guide the organization, the values that differentiate its internal culture, the objectives that define strategy for the next few years, and the goals people are accountable for this quarter.** It's a powerful way to give your team the knowledge they want and need about the organization they are a part of. It gives everyone a little bit of that enterprise orientation that is so critical to your role as CEO.

1-PAGE STRATEGIC PLAN

Mission _____

_____

_____

_____

Vision _____

_____

_____

_____

Differentiating Values

_____ _____

_____ _____

_____ _____

_____ _____

Strategic Objectives (2–3 Years)

_____

_____

_____

_____

_____

_____

Quarterly Goals

_____

_____

_____

_____

_____

Print out copies of the 1-Page Strategic Plan for people to put in their workspaces. Put a copy on the wall of meeting rooms. Place it in shared systems like Microsoft Teams and Slack. Refer to it at all-hands or townhall-style meetings you have. The 1-Page Strategic Plan should become a familiar sight to everyone, as it is the heart of how you deliver predictable performance.

DRIVING GOALS ACROSS THE ORGANIZATION

The company's quarterly goals are the final item on the 1-Page Strategic Plan, but they are just the beginning of a full **goals system**. Without a formal system for helping managers and employees set their own quarterly goals, the CEO risks playing a giant game of telephone, in which company direction is passed down verbally; by the time it makes it to the frontline employee, the meaning has been so contorted as to be unrecognizable. Then the CEO is surprised when they find out employees aren't accomplishing the key initiatives. Additionally, without a strong goals system, the CEO is not getting direct information from the people who know the most about what is happening on the front lines of the business.

The 1-Page Strategic Plan is the first part of such a system. The follow-through should be a quarterly goal-setting practice that cascades from the company's goals to goals for each executive, manager, and employee. This gives people line-of-sight visibility into how their goals and objectives tie to the goals and objectives of the organization as a whole. It is a primary responsibility of management to translate for employees how individual contributions through day-to-day work tie into the goals and objectives of the organization.

In 1-on-1s with your executives, ask them to define quarterly goals for their group, using the company goals as a starting point. Once established, these goals should be shared vertically with employees in that executive's department and horizontally with leaders of the other departments. From there, the cascade continues. Within a couple of weeks of the start of the quarter, everyone in the organization should have a small set of well-defined, strategically aligned goals that show them how their performance ties up and into the big picture of the company.

If your organization's current goal-setting practice is rudimentary or nonexistent, it will take some time to build your system. We encourage you to go slow and steady. If you can establish clear and inspiring goals at the corporate level that link to goals at the department level, you will have put yourself several steps ahead of the vast majority of your competitors. If you are interested in a documented process and software for enabling a companywide goal system, you are welcome to use a software tool I developed specifically to help CEOs drive this process. You can visit AmericanCEO.com/software to get in touch with us and begin using the tool free of charge.

ASK TWO POWER QUESTIONS

Once everyone in the organization has goals and objectives, it is up to you to monitor performance in a way that identifies problems as early as possible. This is an area where many CEOs miss the forest for the trees; they lose their enterprise orientation and fall back into task management. Modern organizations produce copious amounts of data, resulting in "dashboards" that look like something from the cockpit of a commercial airliner. The data may be interesting, but it's not directly tied to any destination and therefore cannot answer the CEO's fundamental question: Are we going to get where we need to go on time?

Instead of monitoring all the gauges, the CEO must learn to trust their executives with the data and surface the insight that will answer that question. We have found that a combination of two power questions can accomplish this with remarkable efficiency. Once your quarterly goals are in place, we encourage you to use these two questions on a weekly basis. Together, they ensure that your organization is on track to deliver performance predictably—and that you are aware early when it is not. This predictability is under-appreciated by most CEOs, but it is what your board and shareholders most want to see. If you can deliver on your commitments in a steady drumbeat and alert stakeholders early when a goal *won't* be met, you will be fully meeting your responsibility to deliver performance.

The two power questions came to life after I had led many meetings that offered little in the way of information about future performance. As you know, in a typical weekly operations meeting, the CEO and executives discuss what's going on in all the primary areas of the organization. Early in my career, I would ask my executives to submit their department's data first thing on Monday morning. Each would usually send over three to five pages of data, which would be compiled into a thirty- to fifty-page report by late morning so I could review it before our 1:00 p.m. operations meeting. Then, in the meeting, we would discuss the report in a roundtable, with each executive recounting what had happened in their area that week.

After a while, I noticed two problems with this approach. One, it became obvious that when one executive was talking in this meeting, most of the others were checked out and just waiting for their turn to talk—or for the meeting to end. Because the data was so segmented and specialized, it held no interest for the other leaders at the table. In effect, it was a series of 1-on-1s that dragged on while other executives surreptitiously caught up on email. The second problem was that we spent most of our time talking about the sales forecast. That was the only thing everybody seemed to be interested in. Though sales was important, it was just one of six functional areas. I realized that the reason we spent so much of our time on sales was because they provided a forecast and thus visibility into the future. Everybody else was offering data about what had happened in the past week. But the CEO can't drive the bus using data about the past; you drive the bus by looking forward through the windshield, by looking into the future. I realized that we needed something different. (Since this realization, I've witnessed the same issue in many board meetings I have attended as a director. It's the same fifty-page reports and the same domination of the meeting by sales.)

With input from a few smart employees, we eventually developed two power questions that would help me, as CEO, understand where we were headed. I then posed these questions to the executive responsible for the goal each week. The first questions is: **How likely are you to achieve this goal on time?** In a typical meeting, questions about goals are past-oriented. They might be about what percentage is done, or what's happened on that goal this week. This Likelihood question, instead, subtly but significantly shifts the question toward the future, asking the owner of the goal for a *prediction* of whether they will achieve it on time. The question works for a few reasons. One, it puts the onus on the executive to interpret the data produced by their own department to arrive at a prediction. This bypasses the need for you to pore over long reports and do your own interpretation. The Likelihood question cuts to the chase: What does this mean for the goals we said were important? This is what you, the CEO, need to know to manage performance at the enterprise level. Sometimes only the goal owner themselves can give you this insight.

This is important because a goal might appear to be 90 percent of the way there, but the team could have no idea how the last 10 percent will be accomplished. And if a goal isn't going to be met, you need to know early. This allows you to facilitate communication with appropriate stakeholders, whether it's the other internal teams with dependencies on that goal or perhaps your board who should be alerted that a revenue goal may be missed.

Another benefit of the Likelihood question is that it asks the goal owner to take accountability for the goal. If they make a weekly prediction—ranging from Very Unlikely to Very Likely—on whether the goal will be achieved, you have reinforced their ownership of the goal and their own motivation to be accurate in their prediction.

There is one facet of performance that the Likelihood question can overlook, however, which is the quality of the work itself. If your oversight of goals only looks at on-time achievement, you could be missing trade-offs made to reach the goal. For example, did your engineering team deliver the product to schedule even though it's held together with duct tape and a prayer? Or did your sales team meet their bookings goal at the expense of a totally drained pipeline? Or maybe while they will hit the number this quarter, the type of deals they are selling are low margin or in some other way not attractive. You can surface issues like these by pairing the Likelihood question with the Quality question: **How do you feel about the quality of the work done so far?** Ask the goal owner to give you a quick rating on a 1–5 scale.

By asking these two simple but powerful questions, you can drive predictable performance in your organization without getting bogged down in reams of data that don't answer the question you are most concerned with: Are we going to hit the goals that I promised the board to deliver in the given quarter?

OPERATING RHYTHM

With your 1-Page Strategic Plan in place, your team equipped with goals for the quarter, and the two power questions in your back pocket, you can begin a steady operating rhythm that keeps execution on track. A good operating rhythm for most CEOs includes the following components.

Quarterly Planning

At the end of each quarter, company-level quarterly goals should be closed out with the executive team. Go through each goal, marking them Achieved or Not Achieved. Spend some time on lessons learned from both the wins and losses. For missed goals, what implications does this have for the future? Should the goal be reset for the next quarter, or has the plan changed? Then it is time to set new goals for the coming quarter, as discussed previously. Don't forget to update the 1-Page Strategic Plan with these goals and provide a new copy to all employees.

Weekly Operations Meeting

The weekly meeting of your executive team is instrumental to company performance. Often, it's the only time the C-suite is gathered together in the same room and their only chance to step out of the day-to-day tactical mindset to examine issues from the organizational level.

As you lead the weekly operations meeting, maintain your enterprise orientation and encourage the executives to adopt a similar multifunctional perspective. Instead of having executives take turns discussing progress in their areas, lead a review of the company's quarterly goals, focusing on the two power questions. If the first objective for the quarter is to drive $20 million in revenue, the CEO begins a discussion of any issues around that target. Is it still likely to be achieved? Is the quality of the work holding up? Product may speak up to say that a ship date has been delayed. Marketing may flag a slowing down of pipeline. HR might comment about a key sales rep who quit. Customer Support might bring up a service issue that could impede future sales. Finance might let the team know that there is not enough inventory to fill certain orders. Crucially, the whole team rises above the department level to engage in a discussion of shared future outcomes. This is also the opportunity to ask if any department needs help from another department.

This approach not only facilitates real collaboration but also decreases time spent in meetings. I've run both billion-dollar and ten-million-dollar companies with this approach and kept the meeting run time to about thirty minutes. (That's a huge cut from those early operations meetings that often ran on for two hours, despite attendees being less engaged and focused.) When problems do come up in your weekly operations meeting, the CEO should assign out the relevant action items and then follow up next week. If further problem solving is needed or if people start down a rabbit hole, set a different meeting that includes only the relevant attendees.

1-on-1 Meetings

Another weekly element of your operating rhythm should be 1-on-1 meetings with your executives and any other direct reports. Many CEOs set these but frequently reschedule them when an urgent (or urgent-seeming) issue arises. When this happens repeatedly, it communicates to the executive that your time together isn't very important. Do your best to stick with the rhythm and never let more than two weeks pass without a 1-on-1 with each executive.

Because both your and your executives' time is highly valuable, strive to keep your 1-on-1s purposeful, not letting them devolve into aimless chit-chat sessions. Thirty minutes is enough for most 1-on-1s, though if you have a newly onboarded executive, you may spend longer with them initially as you help them acclimate to the role and the culture.

As CEO, what should you cover in the 1-on-1? We recommend structuring 1-on-1s around three topics. The first topic is the general operation of the executive's area as measured by their key performance indicators (KPIs). We will discuss why and how to set KPIs with executives in a moment. The idea is to check in on the fundamental success measures of that executive's part of the business. The second topic is the executive's quarterly goals; this may overlap somewhat with the previous topic, as you and the executive may have decided to set a quarterly goal around one of their KPIs. For this part of the 1-on-1, pull out your two power questions. For each goal, ask the executive to commit to a likelihood rating of achievement by end of quarter, and ask them how they feel about the quality of work being done. The third topic of the 1-on-1 is coaching. As discussed in Part I, you serve a coaching role for each of your direct reports, even if they are more proficient in certain functional areas than you are. Following the guidelines covered in the previous section on coaching, strive to understand where they want to go in their career, learn about the skills they hope to develop, and reflect back to them anything you have observed that could help them grow.

A further word about giving feedback is warranted, as it requires a delicate balance. For many CEOs, the first impulse when they notice an issue with one of their executives is to avoid talking about it, especially to the executive themselves. The CEO may not want to come across as harsh or hurt anyone's feeling, so they just hope the issue will go away on its own. This approach does a huge disservice to the organization and to the executive in question. If there is an issue, whether it's performance-based, personality-based, or otherwise, it is incumbent upon you to address it directly and quickly rather than making yourself comfortable by hiding from it. But the other side of this balance is not simply harping on the executive's perceived weaknesses or past errors when you do address the issue. If you sit down in a 1-on-1, take a deep breath, and tell your head of human resources all the ways her presentation to the board last week didn't live up to expectations, you're likely to create frustration, if not panic, in that leader. After all, what's done is done—how are they supposed to fix it now? **A better approach is** *feedforward.* When you offer feedforward, you tell the person what they might do differently in the future to produce a better outcome. Rather than giving a highlight reel of the failures of that bad presentation, tell the HR head what they might change up next time to really engage and impress the board. Before I learned to give feedforward, I had a few situations where people thought I was about to fire them based on the blunt feedback I gave them, even though this wasn't my intention at all. Feedforward allows you to honestly address issues while creating a positive path forward. That makes it a very handy tool in 1-on-1s.

Active listening is also critical in 1-on-1s. Your ability to pay close attention to what the executive is saying, without interruption, determines a huge percentage of the meeting's success. Close your computer and put aside your phone. Remember the adage about how we have two ears and one mouth; using them in about that ratio is appropriate in the 1-on-1.

Finally, remember the Platinum Rule and approach the 1-on-1 in a manner that fits with the executive's personality. It's a good idea to review personality data about the executive before 1-on-1s, including their DISC type, their top Clifton-Strengths themes, and their User Manual. This reminds you how that executive views the world and helps you treat them in a way that makes them most productive and engaged.

Quarterly Performance Reviews

You may think of quarterly performance reviews as an administrative responsibility in the domain of human resources. However, we encourage you to hold a quarterly review with each of your executives. This can essentially be a more formal version of the weekly 1-on-1, but be sure you do two things as part of the review.

First, close out the executive's quarterly goals with them, similar to how you closed out the company's quarterly goals. Discuss whether each one was achieved and what lessons or actions need to be taken. Were the executive's predictions—their responses to the Likelihood question—accurate over the quarter? For poor performers, you will see a consistent pattern of setting goals, predicting they will achieve them, and then failing to achieve those goals.

The outcome of the executive's goals, along with the accuracy of their predictions, forms the primary content of the review. Thanks to the goals you set with the executive and your weekly conversations about them, you have relevant data to review on their performance. It's a sharp contrast to most performance reviews, where the manager grades their employee on subjective measures, often trying to remember and summarize events that took place over the course of a whole year.

The second part of the review is your own confidential rating of the executive's performance on an A-B-C scale. To create a standard for how individuals' work performance is rated across the organization, we have long recommended that companies implement this simple A-B-C rating system. Under the system, managers rate their direct reports as an A, B, or C each quarter. These ratings are not seen by the employees being rated but are visible up the management chain. This gives the CEO, human resources, and other leaders an updated view of where A-players sit throughout the organization. It also shows them where the C-players are—the people who need to be trained up, relocated, or removed from the organization.

The exercise of managers rating their direct reports A, B, or C should begin with you, the CEO. How would you rate your executives on their performance this quarter? You can consider the following criteria as you rate the executive. Managers throughout the company should follow the same guideline.

- **A-players** are exceptional contributors to long-term profitability because they are among the top 15 percent of their peers throughout the industry. A-players also contribute to competitive advantage by being aligned with and supporting the values of the organization.

- **B-players** are between the top 15 percent and 50 percent of performers throughout the industry in their current roles. B-players are valuable contributors who consistently meet and may exceed expectations in many areas of performance. Management's responsibility is to grow them into A-players in their current roles or move them into roles that best utilize their strengths.

- **C-players** put the company at a competitive disadvantage by being below average relative to their peers at principal competitors. Management's responsibility is to rapidly develop them in their current role or get them into a role where they can be an A-player. If this cannot be done in a timely manner, the individual should not be retained.

If you truly believe that all your executives are A-players, the company should be delivering runaway results every quarter. More likely you have one or two A-players, several B-players, and potentially a C-player or two.

A strong, steady operating rhythm is the CEO's best tool for delivering predictable performance. It can take a while to build. Much of it is about simple discipline in setting goals, reviewing them weekly, having the uncomfortable conversations, and thinking ahead.

The other benefit of a strong operating rhythm is that it sets the tone for all other managers in the organization. As I discuss extensively in my previous book, *The Manager's Playbook*, once a company grows past the startup phase, a strong slate of people managers is absolutely vital for the health of the business. The managers at your company determine how engaged and motivated people are, how well you can hang on to talent, and whether employees are applying their time and effort to the most business-relevant work. Every manager in your organization should operate in sync with the rhythm you set from the top. They, too, should be setting and closing out quarterly goals, holding weekly team meetings and 1-on-1s, asking the two power questions, and reviewing employee performance at the end of the quarter. By keeping up your own operating rhythm, you set an example for everyone else in a management role.

EXECUTIVE PERFORMANCE PROFILES

We recommend one final tool to help you deliver performance: work with each of your direct reports to write an **Executive Performance Profile**. This is a document that clarifies the executive's responsibilities, scope of authority, KPIs, and goals for the quarter; it is essentially a condensed job description for the executive. See p. 167 for a sample. We recommend putting these in place for each executive on your team, then revisiting and updating on a quarterly basis.

The Executive Performance Profile should include:

- **Responsibility.** This is a concise statement of the business value created by the executive in their role. You can think of it as a statement of what the executive *owns*, whether that's an outcome, a business function, or a relationship.

- **Authority.** This specifies the decisions the executive can make and the actions the executive can take without input from the CEO. It may include, for example, a dollar amount the executive can spend without prior approval from you. Remember that decisions "below the waterline" should be made by the executive.

- **Key Performance Indicators (KPIs).** These are the three to five core metrics that define whether the executive and their department are successful. Ensure that they align with the Responsibilities above.

- **Quarterly Goals.** These are the four to six SMART goals the executive and their department commit to for the quarter. They should align with the company' quarterly goals.

- **Personality Data.** It's a good idea to include personality assessment data like DISC type and CliftonStrengths as a reminder for yourself and others.

In CEO training sessions, we often have attendees pick one of their current direct reports and fill out their Executive Performance Profile. We then ask them to go back to the office and have the executive write their own profile. The CEO and executive then compare notes—and are often surprised by how different some of their conceptions are, especially as it relates to what they are responsible for. That's part of the value of the Executive Performance Profile. In addition to reinforcing what's most important for the executive, it also keeps the CEO and executive on the same page—literally!

Of the items on the Executive Performance Profile, the KPIs tend to require the most thought. The best way to arrive at great KPIs is to have conversations with the executive where you continue to ask *why* certain metrics best reflect the performance of the department. Ask questions like "Why does this department exist?" and "What business value does this department need to create?" Once the KPIs are agreed upon, the CEO should ask the executive to track them and make them available—preferably to the whole organization. In some companies I've run, we had all department heads put their KPIs on a bulletin board outside their office; in others, we've used shared software for this purpose.

At NetQoS, whenever a new executive started working for me, I would ask them to identify three to five KPIs that show they are doing a good job. One of these conversations changed the whole trajectory of the company. When I asked a new sales director how we should measure sales, he said "Revenue." That's a pretty clear and obvious KPI for a sales director, and one we would indeed track together. But I also wanted to dig deeper and get at something that more directly reflected his performance in his role. We discussed the weaknesses of revenue as a KPI in this regard. For one, if engineering built a bad product and he couldn't sell it, the lack of revenue didn't make him a bad salesperson. Same if the economy tanked and he couldn't sell.

"How long will it take to sell this product from the first time you talk to a customer?" I asked the sales director.

"This is a big-ticket item," he said, "so it will have to go through a lot of approvals in the organization. In all, it will probably take five to six months for the deal to close."

We realized that this meant at the beginning of the quarter, he would already know about every deal that was likely to close that quarter. If he was running a really good sales process and understood how our customer buys, he ought to be able to predict with some accuracy how much he would close in that period—barring some kind of sudden change mid-quarter. We decided that his top KPI would not be revenue but *accuracy of sales forecasting*.

What difference did this make? A big one. Had we established revenue as his top KPI, this sales director would likely have taken very different actions. He'd want to bring on new salespeople every week to land more deals. Or he'd want to reduce the price of the product to increase volume of sales, promote new features that may be hard to deliver—anything that would help him chase pure revenue. Instead, with accuracy of sales forecasting as his touchstone, he went and built a sales process. He collected data, such as how many demos turned into purchases, and used this to refine his revenue predictions each quarter. He surveyed customers about what helped them along in the sales process, and found that the professionalism of the sales team was their number-one reason for buying from our company. Accordingly, he trained new salespeople for two months before letting them talk to a customer so they wouldn't make mistakes, and required them to pass a certification lecture with me in the room. Thanks to this and other tactics, he built a highly predictable sales process that allowed me, as CEO, to see into the future. That one conversation about the most appropriate KPI changed how we approached sales and contributed significantly to thirty-one consecutive quarters of double-digit year-over-year growth. We managed growth without the random ups-and-downs—up 100 percent one quarter, down 50 percent the next—that plague so many scaling companies.

This is the type of breakthrough that can result when you and your leadership team devote proper attention to how performance will be measured, whether at the individual, department, or company level.

EXECUTIVE PERFORMANCE PROFILE

Name: Joel Trammell

Title: VP Customer Service

Responsibility: VP Customer Service is responsible for ensuring the highest possible level of customer satisfaction with available resources.

Authority: VP Customer Service is authorized to approve all departmental budgeted expense items or unbudgeted items less than $5,000.

Key Performance Indicators:

1. Customer satisfaction as measured by NPS
2. Percentage of customers renewing maintenance
3. Number of customer referrals

Q1 Goals:

1. Increase NPS score from 40 to 45
2. Reach 90% customer renewals within the quarter
3. Provide five customer referrals to sales and marketing
4. Reduce average trouble ticket solution time to 3 hours

DISC Type: Dc

CliftonStrengths: Learner, Relator, Competition, Intellection, Responsibility

DELIVER PERFORMANCE: BUILD YOUR PLAYBOOK

- **Create your 1-Page Strategic Plan.** This should include:

  - The mission, vision, and differentiating values you created previously

  - Strategic objectives for the next two to three years

  - Company goals for the next quarter

- **Distribute the 1-Page Strategic Plan to the entire company.** This includes everyone from your executives to frontline employees. Share it digitally and in print. Encourage people to display it in their workspaces.

- **Create Executive Performance Profiles for each of your direct reports.** Include specific quarterly goals for each executive.

- **Establish your operating rhythm.** Schedule weekly operations meetings, weekly 1-on-1s with each of your executives, and quarterly performance reviews. Ensure that you are using the two power questions weekly in operations meetings and 1-on-1s. Schedule quarterly planning sessions out into the future, two weeks before the beginning of the next quarter.

THE ORGANIZATIONAL MATURITY MODEL

As the person perched atop the organizational chart and the most visible embodiment of the business, the CEO has always had a significant impact on company outcomes. However, over the past seventy years, researchers have noted a dramatic uptick in how the CEO affects total organizational performance. In the 1950s, the CEO was often regarded as an important but replaceable cog in the machine. They were expected to have at most a modest effect on outcomes. But the latter half of the twentieth century saw the intensification of the so-called "CEO effect," the degree to which the chief executive him- or herself determines overall performance. Today, by comparison to the 1950s, researchers rate the CEO effect as quite strong. In other words, how well you fulfill each of the five CEO responsibilities—and implement the rest of the Chief Executive Operating System—influences the organization in dramatic ways.

In the Organizational Maturity Model on p. 173 you will see how we represent this effect visually. As the CEO masters each responsibility, the organization moves further toward the righthand side. When the CEO has only a weak grasp on the core responsibilities, the company is overall in a confused state:

- The vision is hazy.

- Resources are allocated by whim.

- The culture is chaotic and internally contradictory.

- Decisions get held up at the top.

- Overall performance is random and highly unpredictable.

But as the CEO masters the responsibilities, the organization slowly but surely shifts toward predictable success:

- The vision is clear and acted upon by everyone.

- Resources are allocated to capitalize on opportunities.

- The culture is centered on shared values and mission.

- Smart decisions are made at all levels of the company.

- And there's a full "system of record" for company goals—a place to track these priorities and the weekly predictions against them.

In recent years, we have developed an Organizational Maturity Assessment that measures where a given organization sits on the model. By asking employees to anonymously describe their day-to-day experiences in these five areas, we can estimate the company's maturity—and therefore extrapolate how well the CEO is fulfilling the responsibilities. After administering, analyzing, and presenting many of these surveys, we've made some interesting observations.

The first is that an organization can be simultaneously strong in one area but weak in others. The responsibilities tend to reinforce each other, so it would be rare to see a company at Level 1 in one category but Level 5 for another. However, there can be significant differentials. It is not uncommon for surveys to reflect a company that is for example very disciplined around meeting its stated goals (Deliver Performance) but struggling in the area of culture. This knowledge can help the CEO and executive team understand where attention is needed. Even if just one area is weak, it's worth addressing. In the example above, a company is unlikely to deliver performance over the long run if it continues to have a toxic or confused culture.

The second observation we've made is that Level 3 is a common place for even outwardly successful companies to end up on the Organizational Maturity Model. If a company is experiencing Level 4, it may think it's in business nirvana—and it probably is several tiers above its competitors. But true Level 5 is a rarity. Level 5 is the ideal level of maturity that is seldom attained but worth striving for.

The third observation we've made is that perceptions of the company's maturity vary across groups. We typically segment the Organizational Maturity Assessment so we can tease out the perspectives of the CEO, the executive leadership team, middle managers, and employees at large. While there is usually general consensus across groups, disparities are not infrequent and offer a fascinating starting point for group discussion. For example, we've seen organizations in which executives think the vision and strategy is crystal clear, even though the rank and file think it's anything but. We've also seen CEOs who give themselves low marks in certain areas only to find that their team disagrees and thinks they are doing an excellent job in those same areas. Presenting these disparities often leads to a refreshing level of insight and positive realignment.

If you are interested in having your company take the Organizational Maturity Assessment, please reach out to us at info@ AmericanCEO.com. In addition to estimating your company's maturity level in the five areas, we also present individual insights from the survey and offer customized suggestions. In high-trust organizations especially, employees are often willing to add candid comments as part of the survey. It's a little like a 360-degree evaluation for your company as a whole, and we've seen it lead to perspective-shifting insights for CEOs and their teams.

ORGANIZATIONAL MATURITY MODEL

Maturity Level

CEO Responsibilities	Confused	Described	Declared	Influenced	Predictable
Deliver Performance	Random performance	Basic metrics	Broad metrics	Comprehensive metrics	Full system of record
Make Decisions	CEO is decision bottleneck	Executive team makes decisions	Decisions driven by processes	Some decisions made by the right people	Right people make the right decisions
Build a Decision-Making Organization	Multiple conflicting cultures	Values are stated but not embraced	Rules-based culture	Engaged employees	Mission first
Provide the Resources	Random hiring and spending	Reactive hiring and spending	Budget-based allocation	Forward-looking allocation	Opportunity-driven allocation
Own the Vision	CEO has an idea	Vision shared with chosen few	Majority understand vision	Everyone knows the story	Everyone owns and acts on the story

Management | Leadership | Coaching

PART III
YOU

THE 6 ESSENTIAL SKILLS OF THE CEO

Just about any skill you possess can be applied to the CEO job somehow. However, if you want to master the role, there are a few fundamental skills that tend to matter most. When we work with CEOs to implement the Chief Executive Operating System, we focus on the following six. Your first opportunity is to ensure you have basic proficiency in these skills. Once you do, you can embark on the lifelong journey of developing them to your maximum potential.

SKILL 1: AUTHENTIC AND TRANSPARENT COMMUNICATION

The first skill of the CEO—the fundamental ability underlying all the others—is good communication. From company townhalls to press interviews to 1-on-1s, the CEO is required to apply communication skills almost continuously. The two words you want people to use most when describing your communication are *authentic* and *transparent*.

First, **authentic**: The CEO role is the most personal job in the organization, making authenticity in how you communicate critical. As CEO, it's very hard to put on different faces and personas, because you are under scrutiny basically all the time. Any inconsistencies will be noticed, discussed, and possibly misinterpreted. If you say one thing to one group but then say something contradictory to another, word will get around. Even when speaking to very different audiences—the board, the executive team, your workforce at large, your customers—your communication must reflect your authentic character.

Most CEOs fail to appreciate just how much attention is paid to everything they say and do. This is why your words and actions must come from an authentic place—they have to reflect who you actually are and what you actually believe. Of course, this isn't an excuse for you to indulge your bad habits. If you have a temper problem and occasionally fly off the handle, it does no good to say that you were just being your authentic self. You'll just be seen as being authentically a jerk. Instead, pull from your best true self as you communicate, following your inner compass, not projecting who you think people want you to be.

The second word you want people to use when describing your communication is **transparent**. Note that transparency is different from honesty. Honesty implies that if asked a question, you will tell the truth. But you can hide information if you're not asked the right question and still declare yourself honest. Transparency brings a different standard: It means you will provide all the pertinent information even if you aren't explicitly asked about it, and even if it is uncomfortable.

There are only a few situations where it makes sense for the

CEO to withhold information from employees. The most obvious is personal information about the health and performance of individual employees. Another involves any information with legal ramifications, such as being in negotiations with a public company to be acquired. Other than these, the great majority of information about the business can and should be communicated to everybody.

Communicating about the true state of the business—including development of products and services, the state of the sales activity, and strategy for the future—is part of this transparent communication. If you think that your employees "can't handle the truth," think again: They can, and you owe them the truth. When it comes to sharing financial information about the business with employees, you may need to offer education and context so they can fully understand, as Jack Stack discusses in *The Great Game of Business*. Given that most employees, even most CEOs, are not skilled at reading financial statements, simply providing a financial statement will not offer a lot of transparent value.

Communicating authentically and transparently to employees, the board, owners, and other stakeholders is relatively easy when things are going well. The challenge is when things aren't. In this situation, many CEOs will slow down their communication, only sharing their true feelings with a small inner circle, if with anyone. But by avoiding that communication, we're not sparing others from the truth; in reality, we're being selfish as leaders. A CEO might convince themselves that everything will be great, but really they don't want to say things like "We had a bad quarter," "We lost a big customer," or "We won't have the resources to fund payroll in three months." But these problems can only be ignored for so long. If the CEO continues to say that everything is great and then suddenly announces a layoff one Friday, employees will feel betrayed, and you will have lost credibility with everyone remaining. Anytime you are not transparent and authentic in your communication, you run the risk of being found out at a later date and having all trust destroyed.

How often do different groups—frontline employees, middle managers, executives, board members, owners, shareholders, customers, etc.—hear from you personally? What touchpoints might you want to add? And how can you make your communication through those touchpoints both authentic and transparent?

A final note about communication. Good communication in the CEO role requires repetition. People need to hear a message many times before it sinks in. You may feel strange at first saying the same things over and over again, but don't worry—it's required. In fact, we recommend identifying a few critical themes you want people to internalize and honing them into "sayings" that you can use often. They may relate to the company's mission and vision, a value of the organization or of yourself as a leader, a particular objective or goal, or a behavior or attitude you want to encourage among the workforce. People should know these sayings and hear them often from you. As Marc Cenedella, CEO of the job site TheLadders .com, puts it, "Until they start making jokes about how often you repeat it, they haven't internalized it."

SKILL 2: HOLDING PEOPLE ACCOUNTABLE

One of the most frequent questions we get from executives, including CEOs, is "How do I hold employees accountable?"

The word *accountability* is scary, though, especially to

employees. When we say "Someone needs to be held account-able," we usually mean that someone should be fired. The CEO who wants to hold someone accountable isn't always thinking about showing someone the door, but they are typically frus-trated that the organization hasn't delivered. They think they said, or at least implied, what needed to be done—and now it isn't done! What's the deal?

Nine times out of ten, the CEO in this situation failed to set clear expectations, which will make any efforts to "hold someone accountable" futile. In reality, accountability is a two-part pro-cess: it requires the CEO to have the *clarity* to establish a shared understanding of what needs to be done with each executive and then the *courage* to level with the executive should they fail to meet those shared expectations.

Unless each of your executives has specific, objective mea-surements by which to evaluate their performance, it's almost impossible to hold them accountable. Without them, the execu-tive can too easily point to someone else's failure, say they didn't understand what you wanted or that the goal wasn't clear. Thus, the CEO who excels in the skill of accountability ensures that every executive on the team knows these three to five KPIs, as discussed in Responsibility 5 (Deliver Performance).

With clarity created, you can enforce the second part of the accountability equation: the courage to *show the executive objective reality* when expectations aren't met. We like the phrase "showing them objective reality" better than "holding them accountable" here, because that's really what you're doing: you're reinforcing to them that, based on the standards set, there's a measurable differential in expectation and performance. Many times, this won't be the executive's fault per se. But no matter what the case, the difficult conversation needs to be had. Many

CEOs, not wanting to be negative, act as if the established measurements no longer matter and forge on with new metrics. But this isn't real accountability. Bring out your authentic, transparent communication and discuss the objective reality that performance isn't what you agreed to aim for. Only once this reality is confronted can you move on to productive solutions.

SKILL 3: CURIOSITY

Is curiosity really a skill? We think so. It's something that the CEO can and should actively cultivate in themselves. A CEO who is on a continuous mission to learn more and understand more is uniquely positioned to lead their organization through all sorts of situations.

If you are only interested in a few narrow aspects of your business, the organization is likely to suffer. Each of the six areas we discussed in Part I—sales, marketing, product; customers, employees, shareholders—deserves attention and curiosity from you. How do these functions operate? What are their challenges? Why do your customers buy? Why do employees come work for you? Why do investors invest in you? When the CEO feeds their curiosity about these things, they are able to mentally integrate them into a rich overall picture of the organization.

This curiosity drives all kinds of good outcomes. You'll be better able to set performance goals with executives, more confident in understanding each department's output, more engaging in your communication to various stakeholders. And, by continuously learning about each corner of the organization, you bolster the three Cs of leadership we talked about before: you grow your competence, you're able to speak more credibly, and most important, you show people you care.

SKILL 4: DECISION MAKING

In Part II, we discussed your responsibility to build a decision-making organization. When you have done this effectively, your executives, managers, and frontline employees will make swift decisions informed by the overall strategy and values of the organization.

But that still leaves you to make the most consequential decisions facing the organization. As we have discussed, the quality and speed of your decisions determines how fast the organization can move. Keeping the following principles in mind won't help you get every decision right, but they will give you a better batting average, more confidence, and greater buy-in from the organization.

1. **Don't make every decision.** Only inexperienced CEOs take on every decision, no matter how small. The CEO should make the decision on issues that will significantly impact all areas of the business, such as those around strategy and resource allocation. Trust your people. Don't allow them to dump a decision on you if they have the expertise, responsibility, and authority to handle it.

2. **Assign a devil's advocate.** Some decisions—such as making a major acquisition, selling your company, or choosing an equity financing partner—are almost impossible to reverse and carry tremendous risk. Careful analysis and thorough discussion are critical. Assign a senior person to play devil's advocate, testing conclusions and identifying any weaknesses. (As mentioned in Part II, these irreversible decisions typically comprise less than 5 percent of decisions you will make.)

3. **Act swiftly.** Effective CEOs are comfortable making decisions with incomplete information. If you wait for all the information before making a decision—and you can never have *all* the information—you risk losing valuable momentum. Resist the urge to use ongoing data collection to put off the decision. Not making a decision is in itself a decision, and usually not the best one.

4. **Communicate the "what" and the "why."** Once you make a decision, people need to hear about it from you. Start by telling them *what* exactly was decided. What does this decision mean for them? What will it affect in daily operations? Along with the what, communicate the *why*. Employees, especially the brightest, want to know the reasoning behind the decision and why you, the CEO, feel it is the best move. Hearing this from you not only helps people buy into the decision that was made— it also models the type of thoughtful decision making they themselves should be engaged in.

5. **Hold postmortems.** It's a good idea to hold formal postmortems on significant company decisions several months after they are made. You will need to create a culture where people are comfortable speaking up if they believe the current course of action isn't working out. These official postmortems should be paired with continuous monitoring of key metrics surrounding the decision.

6. **Reverse bad decisions quickly.** Admitting failure is difficult, but refusing to acknowledge that you made a bad decisions is dangerous. If all evidence from your postmortems and monitoring points to the decision not being the right one, it's time to steer in a different direction.

7. **Find good advisors.** Though you alone are responsible for top-level decisions in the organization, it's wise to have people you trust to act as a sounding board. Whether it is a longtime mentor or a peer advisory group you join, good advisors can help you identify blind spots in your decision making, give insights from industries and organizations outside your own, and offer emotional support in a responsibility that can sometimes feel quite lonely.

8. **Understand common decision-making biases.** Even the most brilliant humans are prone to biases that can skew decision making—yes, even you. For a good primer on this, we recommend Chip and Dan Heath's *Decisive: How to Make Better Choices in Life and Work*. They walk through four predictable "villains" of good decision making: narrow framing, confirmation bias, short-term emotion, and overconfidence about the future.

SKILL 5: PRODUCTIVITY

The next skill a CEO must cultivate is the ability to be consistently productive. With a job where everyone wants some of your time and where there always seems to be a fire to put out, it's easy to stay busy. But mere busy-ness is not the same as productivity. In fact, staying reactively busy all day is one of the laziest ways to do the CEO job.

The organization relies on you to anticipate the future and proactively position it for success. You must identify the activities where you bring the most value and protect time for doing the things only the CEO can do. Much of the time, the emergency of the day isn't it. Here is a simple guide: Most of your activities should relate back to the five key responsibilities we just covered.

To find out whether you're spending your time wisely, start with an audit of a workweek. For one week, log your activity in fifteen-minute increments—all the meetings and discussions, all the direct tasks you work on, any writing and reading you do, and your thinking time. Review your log at the end of each day of that week: Which activities were truly important? Which did you do just because they showed up on your desk? Which created some kind of business value? Which could have been done by someone else?

You may have heard of the Eisenhower matrix, based on a concept developed by the United States' thirty-fourth president. It's a simple and effective tool for prioritizing tasks according to their urgency and importance. You can categorize the activities in your log in the below framework, and use it to triage issues as they come up throughout your day:

	URGENT	**NOT URGENT**
IMPORTANT	**DO** Tasks that require timely action and your expertise and support	**SCHEDULE** Tasks that have unclear deadlines but that likely contribute to long-term success
NOT IMPORTANT	**DELEGATE** Tasks that require timely action but that do not require your input	**DELETE** Tasks that are unnecessary distractions

In working with CEOs on this exercise, we find that a surprising amount of tasks end up in the Delete box. In other words, much of what the chief executive spends time on could be moved off their plate without any negative impact to the organization. One popular time-wasting task is attending unnecessary meetings, including the CEO traveling long distances for a meeting that's either brief, inconsequential, or both. Another common waste of time for CEOs is collecting and analyzing information about the various functions of the business. This often results when the CEO hasn't set clear goals and measurements with their department heads, as discussed previously. Because the CEO has no sense of what data is most critical and predictive of success, they hope that their personal analysis of the data will turn up the answer to a business problem. In this case, a far better use of the CEO's time is talking through the data with key people in the department. That is exhibiting real curiosity and trying to learn from the expertise of your team. Combing through the data by yourself is, more often than not, a distraction.

The tasks in the Schedule box of the Eisenhower matrix—the ones that are important but don't feel urgent—are often neglected by the CEO. However, these tasks can have huge value for the organization, so the CEO must carefully protect time for them. They include things like strategic planning, analysis of future risks and opportunities, learning on key topics, and building a talent pipeline for the organization. If the CEO doesn't actually schedule time for these things, they tend to get pushed off into infinity.

Finally, effective CEOs make liberal use of the Delegate box. Especially when leading an organization as it scales up from startup phase, the CEO may struggle to give up tasks they are used to do doing. But delegation is a good idea for at least two reasons. First, it frees up your time and increases the scalability of the organization. As with decision making, if the CEO tries to maintain control of hands-on tasks, their plate is full of non-strategic work and they can become a bottleneck. Second, delegation builds trust with your employees: Nothing says you have faith in them like handing them ownership of something, especially a significant project. Recall that one of the top motivators of employees is *responsibility*. If you can get past your impulse to do things yourself, delegation is a win-win for you and your team. You get more time; they get more responsibility and a chance to develop their skills.

Delegating properly does require time and care. To maximize the likelihood that the employee will carry out the task successfully, your instructions must be precise. If you give unclear direction and the employee fails at the task, the result can be a cycle of blaming the employee as incompetent and micromanaging future tasks.

Anytime you delegate a task, you must answer the three questions that pertain to the three CEO tools: What needs to be done (management)? Why is this task important (leadership)? And how should this task be done (coaching)? Delegation is similar to what we discussed about the skill of accountability: the more up-front clarity you offer around these three questions, the more successful the delegation process is likely to be. If you do what we call micro-training in the beginning, you end up doing a lot less micro-management later. Too often, we see people given tasks and responsibilities only to have to redo the work once the CEO tells them it wasn't done as expected. Once you have delegated the task, it is wise to check in occasionally. If you just tell them, "Let me know if you have a problem" as you hand the task off, you place the burden on the employee and force them to admit failure before receiving your help. This is abdicating, not delegating. Instead, offer your support proactively.

All the famous, successful CEOs of the past had the same number of minutes in the day that you do. The only difference is how you use those minutes. By establishing your true priorities and delegating well, you can optimize your own productivity and apply it to the work only you can do.

SKILL 6: AWARENESS

The sixth and final skill CEOs must cultivate is their own general awareness—especially their self-awareness.

The foundational thing to maintain awareness of is your own exaggerated importance in the minds of the people who work in the organization. As we discussed previously, for better or for worse, people pay close attention to everything you say and do. That might include telling you what they think you want to hear, picking up subtle but erroneous signals from you, and going out of their way to make a good impression. I remember the story of one executive who was promoted into the CEO role; soon after she was appointed, the brand of scarf she wore to work every day started showing up on women employees across the organization. I've personally had situations where an offhand comment I made was taken far more seriously than I intended and led to actions I never would have imagined. Everything you do as CEO will be scrutinized and amplified. Effective CEOs remain aware of their effect on people and how their position can insulate them from reality.

The next aspect of awareness is something we discussed at length in Part I: understanding your own personality, how it deviates from the normal distribution of the population, and how it meshes with the personalities of the people on your team. Again, writing your User Manual and using CliftonStrengths and DISC is an excellent place to start your journey toward awareness. We have found DISC to be particularly relevant for those in leadership positions. Several DISC assessments will show you a series of spectrums and where you sit on them. This is highly useful information, especially when you sit far to one side of the spectrum. For example, picture a spectrum running from Direct on one side to Expressive on the other. I fall well into the Direct side. I naturally tend to communicate in a matter-of-fact manner without a lot of emotion or detail. So, if I'm interacting with someone who falls on the other end, well over to the Expressive side, I need to be aware that if I'm trying to do them a favor and communicate in the least number of words possible, they may think I'm mad, upset, or don't have time to deal with their questions. With that awareness, I can be a bit more expressive in communicating with them and also make them aware of my tendency toward directness.

This awareness also allows you to ask for assistance from people with different strengths. For example, if I were to write a memo about the departure of an executive from the company, I know my initial version would likely be succinct. I might ask someone on the team who is more expressive to help me flesh it out into something lengthier that will give employees a fuller picture of the situation.

When you develop awareness of the personalities of the people you lead, you can more effectively drive their performance. Some of the best salespeople, for example, are Influence personalities in DISC terms. They need space to speak, because talking helps them clarify their thinking. As a Dominance personality myself, I tend to lack patience with longwinded people, but if I know this about my head of sales, I can accept and support them if they want to talk to me for a few minutes and work out something in their head. As CEOs, we must balance all the leadership styles that help the organization succeed, not just use the ones that are easiest for us.

A final tool we recommend for growing awareness is a 360 review. As you know if you've done one before, these offer you anonymous feedback from people who work with you in different roles in the organization. They can be real eye-openers for the CEO, assuming they have built up enough trust with their teams. Yes, in evaluating the CEO, people may hold back even with anonymity. When you get the results of the 360 review, be open to what you hear and resist any urge to become defensive. Candid feedback is a gift on your journey to awareness.

THE 6 ESSENTIAL SKILLS OF THE CEO: BUILD YOUR PLAYBOOK

- **Write down the sayings that you currently use and the sayings you may want to adopt in the future.**

- **Recall the last five decisions of consequence that you made.** Reflect on whether the decisions could have been made faster, and whether in retrospect the best decision was made.

- **Consider engaging with a CEO coach, trainer, or peer group.** Ask three trusted sources for referrals.

- **Consider going through a 360 review process.** Commit to engaging productively with the feedback you get, both positive and negative.

MINDFULNESS

If you're like most CEOs, your knee-jerk reaction to the concept of "mindfulness" might be dismissive. You're a results-oriented businessperson, not a meditator on a mountain top, right?

But in reality, the mindful approach—living intentionally, deliberately, and with continuously increasing self-awareness—can have tremendously positive effects on the CEO. Mindfulness helps you bring together life and work into a healthy, integrated whole, rather than seeing life and work as competing domains pitted hopelessly against each other.

When you are mindful, you're able to remain centered and calm. You've turned off your autopilot and approach situations with curiosity and creativity. You've rejected the barrage of distractions that keep you from even remembering what you had for dinner last night. You have the energy required to actually *focus*, which is a prerequisite for success in any area, especially in leading your organization as CEO.

In this chapter, we will ask you to consider some foundational concepts related to mindfulness and how your purpose in life intersects with your job as chief executive. A role as consequential and demanding as this one inevitably intrudes into other parts of your life, from family to your own health. It's not just what you do for work; it becomes part of your core identity. Thus, a holistic CEO operating system includes tools for managing the balance between the job you hold and the approach you bring to life.

SUCCESS IS NOT THE SAME AS FULFILLMENT

A person can be successful and not be fulfilled. Plenty of people end up at the pinnacle of their careers without finding an inner sense of contentment, and it's not uncommon to meet chief executives who find themselves in this situation, measuring their inner worth by their outward accomplishments. Outward accomplishments are wonderful, but the thrill of achieving them wears off. They will never be a sustainable source of fulfillment.

Think of a climber who sets their sights on scaling a certain mountain. They decide they will only be happy once they have reached the top. But once the climber gets there and enjoys the view for a few minutes, they are restless, already thinking about the next mountain.

What the climber, like many entrepreneurs and CEOs, has failed to realize is that life happens in the valleys in between the mountain tops. If you are not enjoying the journey along the way, you will not feel happy and fulfilled, and will suffer from fear, stress, frustration, and anxiety. And once you do achieve something big, like securing a CEO role or selling a business, the gratification may only last—what? Weeks? A few days? A couple of hours?

While success is a science with formulas that can be followed, fulfillment is an art and different for each individual.
Most of this book has been about tools and strategies for success
as CEO. Fulfillment as CEO works differently and is highly
dependent on who you are as a person—your personality, values,
upbringing, and unique wiring. As you cultivate mindfulness,
remind yourself that tomorrow's success is just as important as
today's fulfillment. Are you being present as you interact with
employees? Are you recognizing the things you're grateful for?
Are you looking for the tiny wins and opportunities in the present that might lead to bigger things down the road?

Here's one good thing about seeking fulfillment in the
CEO role: In this job, you are uniquely positioned to make a
big impact on other people, and that's one of the fastest ways
to experience fulfillment. To be fulfilled, life has to be about
something greater than ourselves. Your job is ultimately about
serving your shareholders, you customers, and your employees—
even benefitting the economy and world at large. As a CEO,
you have countless ways to make a positive difference in people's
lives from day to day, just as you do in your relationships with
friends, family, and community. This is a much better focus than
constantly chasing the carrot and realizing that in the end, your
life was a "success" that lacked meaning.

Human Being, Not Human Doing

You've probably heard this quote: "You are a human being, not a
human doing." This is another way of saying that your fulfillment
in life is separate from the things you do or achieve. Beingness
has to do with how you show up in the moment to the people
around you. Are you consistently kind and considerate? Are you

a good listener who's appreciative of other people's views? Or does your mind tend to be elsewhere, preoccupied with some future outcome you may or may not control? Who you choose to *be* as CEO has a tremendous impact on the culture of the organization, the trust you build, and the connection people will feel with you.

You have to take responsibility for your fulfillment, because happiness does not come from your circumstances. As the psychotherapist and Buddhist teacher Sylvia Boorstein tells us in the title of one of her books, "Happiness is an inside job." If you rely on something external to make you happy, it can always be taken away from you. But if you can make yourself happy through consistent mindfulness and presence and letting go of your baggage, that's something that can never be taken from you.

And thus fulfillment in life isn't about what you achieve— it's about who you become in the process. At the end of your life, your story and your legacy will not be remembered by the money you earned or the stuff you bought or the deals you closed. You will be remembered by how you made the people closest to you feel, at home and work.

THE ASPIRATIONAL SELF

Someone once told me the definition of hell: on your last day on earth, the person you *could* have become will meet the person you became.

No one is sure who first said this, but we can all imagine the crushing feeling of that encounter. Within each of us is great potential, and it's our choice whether to bring it fully into being. The ancient Greeks used the word *Areté* to refer to the the quest for excellence and achieving your highest potential, moment to moment. What is the life of *Areté* for you? What does this best and most aspirational self look like?

The way to become closer to that aspirational self is to be deliberate, intentional, and mindful. Stephen Covey presents a striking exercise for doing this in *The 7 Habits of Highly Effective People*. The second habit is "Begin with the end in mind," and Covey does mean the ultimate end: death. He asks people to imagine the end of their lives as a means of surfacing what we truly want to be. Take some time in a distraction-free environment to think this through for yourself. Write down the answer to these questions: "The *moment* my friends and family find out that I've died, what do I want them to say or think? And what do I hope is said in my eulogy?" If you have done this exercise before, you will appreciate the value of refining your thoughts and iterating them over time. If you have not, you may be surprised by what you write.

The eulogy exercise is a valuable starting point for reflection and action. What do you need to change for your vision to come true? Is your current approach to your job and to the other parts of your life enough? What do you need to work on first?

Virtually no one wants to be remembered for their job title or bank account. What really matters is how you made people *feel* by your state of being. Reading your eulogy can become part of your weekly personal planning, a vivid tool for helping you remember your true north and what's most important to you.

THREE CATEGORIES OF LIFE

Chunking is a helpful way to simplify concepts for the brain. We chunk phone numbers into three sets of digits, sports into offense and defense, and similarly, you can chunk your life into three categories: *energy*, *work*, and *love*. Though these three areas won't take up equal amounts of time in your day or your week, they are equally important and affect each other. The mindful CEO is aware of all three and the interrelations between them. For example, not having energy is detrimental to work and family, not having work hurts your family, and not having loved ones to share your success with makes work less meaningful. When you're able to improve one area, you also improve the others.

With that in mind, let's look at these three areas. When you are practicing mindfulness, you are deliberate about how you allocate your time across them each day. Practiced over years, this daily intentionality adds up to a life lived according to your deepest priorities.

1. Energy

The energy category of your life deals primarily with your bodily and mental health. If health isn't currently a priority for you, you will struggle to make changes in this area. It's very difficult to change behavior and habits from a purely intellectual perspective. To really change, you must get in touch with *why* you want to be healthy.

We can tell you that it's difficult to perform a job as demanding as that of CEO for very long without taking reasonable care of yourself. You might not think of health as directly related to your performance in the job, but there's a close connection. If you let the stress and pressure of your role push healthy habits to the sideline, it's not just your body that will suffer in the long run—your performance will, too.

An even deeper reason for most people to get healthy

is the quality of time spent with loved ones. Your reason for optimizing your vitality and energy must be pressing and felt emotionally. Otherwise, none of the following common-sense guidance will matter.

Eating

Be on guard for what goes through your mouth. When you take a survival course, the first thing you learn is what *not* to eat in nature, what the poisons are. In modern living, unfortunately, the "what not to eat" list contains some of our favorite foods: sugar, red meat, processed foods, and so on. Each of these greatly affects inflammation, energy, and overall health.

The mind-body connection is undeniable. Feeling crappy physically leads to feeling crappy mentally. Changing how you eat is the single most powerful lever you have for increasing the quality of your energy. There are countless ways of healthy eating, and you have probably learned over your life what works best for you. We simply encourage you to think about the food you eat as connected to all the other areas of your life—including the amount of energy and clarity you bring to the CEO role.

Sleeping

Make getting plenty of sleep a priority. A good night's sleep isn't a luxury; it's an essential for increasing your energy and performance. That's why many top athletes now make sleep an important part of their workout regimen. When you stay up late sending work emails or toss and turn with worry, the resulting lack of rest can cause significant cognitive impairment. That includes lowered self-control, increased irritability, and inability to problem-solve. Not the best recipe for a CEO, right?

You are not exempt from the good-sleep guidelines we've all been taught: Limit your blue-light stimulation from electronics in the evening. Avoid caffeine after lunch and alcohol before bedtime, and don't eat in the two hours before sleep. Get to bed by 10:00 p.m. when possible. Sleep in a cool, dark room. Invest in a quality mattress. Your body, and the people you work with, will thank you.

Moving

Find ways to increase your movement, not just through regular exercise but throughout the day. Take the stairs, use a stand-up desk, take a short walk and stretch every hour—anything that gets your body in motion. The more you move, the more calories you burn, and you also clarify your thinking, lubricate your joints, and boost your energy. As with eating well and sleeping sufficiently, this requires an intentional lifestyle choice.

One form of subtle motion we tend to take for granted is breath. Intentional and deep breathing is one of the most effective ways to stimulate your parasympathetic nervous system and reduce stress. At least once per day, take two minutes for an intentional breathing break. Set a timer. Make it part of your routine. Breathe in for a count of four, hold for a count of four, breathe out for a count of six. Notice how you feel before and after. This exercise is also effective to help you get centered before meetings, to calm yourself in times of stress, and to prepare for situations where you need to be extra sharp. It can also help you fall asleep at night in times when your mind is preoccupied or restless.

2. Work

The bulk of this book has been about the second category of your life: work. Most CEOs we know don't need much help putting adequate time and effort here. However, most of us could bring more intentionality to when and how we do our work.

One powerful tool for doing this is to schedule Deep Work blocks in your week. These are the occasions where you will disconnect from all distractions and spend a significant chunk of time on the work that is most important. Honor this time with yourself for strategic thinking or complex tasks. Unless you schedule and stick to Deep Work blocks, the most significant matters can be trampled on by what feels most urgent.

It's also important to bring a spirit of continuous development to your work. The world, your industry, and your business are constantly changing, and it's incumbent on you to keep up. What you were convinced of a year ago may simply not be true today. Keep building the six skills we talked about in the previous chapter. Push yourself to see things from new perspectives. Seek out new ideas.

Continuous learning can come from attending events, joining industry associations and peer groups, reading books and articles, watching TED Talks—or any other method of learning from people who have interesting knowledge. One unexpected learning strategy we've picked up is meeting with salespeople who have a fast-growing product. This type of person will always be happy to come talk to you about their product and market for half an hour, and it often gives you usable insights, whether or not the product has anything to do with your organization's offerings.

3. Love

For most people, the place of greatest fulfillment is the home. We feel justified working hard, long hours because the work helps take care of the family. The dilemma for many CEOs is that what your family wants most from you is your time. If you sense a disconnect between yourself and loved ones about how much time you're allocating to the Love category of your life, the best path forward is communication. When communication is strong, the relationship is strong.

You can ensure you take time to be with your spouse, children, and other loved ones by scheduling Deep Love blocks in your calendar, just as you would for Deep Work. For the past fifteen years, I (Joel) have blocked out Friday nights on my calendar for family time. This isn't only so I remember to do it—it's to convey to myself, my family, and anyone with access to my calendar that this is a priority. In these Deep Love blocks, you must be completely and fully present, without distractions. Otherwise, it doesn't count. Turn off your phone. If it's on the table or if you can feel its vibration, your attention will be divided. This may feel difficult at first, but know that the ability to be present is like a muscle, something you can build over time.

AM & PM BOOKENDS

In practice, balancing the three categories of your life—energy, work, and love—is tricky. You may not always have control over when urgent matters arise at work and intrude into the other areas.

However, the parts of your day you have the most control over are the bookends: the beginning and the end. Usually, what you do just after getting up and what you do just before going to bed is completely up to you. Creating routines for these mornings and evenings gives you the ability to stay centered and grounded, and to not be swept by the winds of stress and emergency.

Start with your PM bookend, because the key to a good tomorrow is a good evening today. If you stay up too late, eat too much, or otherwise drain your energy in the evening, your whole next day will suffer. Determine what time you need to go to bed to get eight hours of sleep, then subtract thirty to sixty minutes for your PM bookend. In addition to following the previously mentioned recommendations around sleep, we encourage you to implement a "digital sunset"—i.e., create a set time to turn off all electronics. This signals to your body that it's time to slow down and get ready to rest. Otherwise, what you do with your PM bookend is up to you, whatever makes you feel relaxed and restored. It might include stretching, taking a bath, reading a physical book, or journaling.

Once you have enjoyed a restful and rejuvenating sleep, consider your routine for the AM bookend. Ideally, you want the day to already be a success before you have to react to others' urgencies. Select habits and routines you would like to install, things you will do while your mind is clear and undisturbed, before checking news or email. How about meditation, exercise, and/or planning? If you have creative thinking to do or a key decision to make, this is a good time to do it. Setting up a regular AM bookend helps you build the foundation for a confident and intentional day. Once you've done it, you can allow the world in by watching or reading the news, checking email, and getting to work.

REFRAMING STRESS

Stress is a reality of the CEO job, and it can take a toll on your performance and your health if you don't learn to reframe it.

A great amount of stress enters our life through worrying about the future. These feelings are based on a negative visualization of something we don't want to happen, and they can wear us down significantly over time. This is why it's crucial that the CEO learn how to replace those negative visualizations with a visualization of a better, more positive outcome. It's easier said than done, but once you build the muscle and understand how to do it, you will be able to sidestep a huge amount of unnecessary stress.

This process is much like how a person learns to drive a race car. If the car goes into a spin, the driver's natural reaction is to look for the wall so they can avoid hitting it. However, the instructor knows that focusing on the wall inadvertently causes the driver to veer toward it. So, when the instructor pulls the lever that causes the car to go into a spin, she coaches the driver, "*Focus on the open space. That's where you need to go.*" She may even have to physically move the driver's chin toward the open space before they move the car that way and avoid crashing into the wall.

Next time you catch yourself focusing on the wall—the things you don't want to happen—practice replacing it with a focus on the open space. Think about the deal closing, the relationship being built, the milestone being achieved. The more you do it, the faster you will go from negative to positive, and the more likely it is that you will achieve your desired outcome. Remember, *energy flows where focus goes*, so don't focus on what you don't want. Your goal is to accept objective reality without willfully making it worse than it is.

Another source of stress is focusing on past mistakes. The CEO should indeed reflect on the past and understand where they may have gone wrong at points, but do not let this reflection degrade into stress-creating rumination. As the Chinese sage Wu Hsin once said, "Preoccupation with the past is the study of echoes. Preoccupation with the future is the exercise of imagination."

In the final analysis, stress is a form of fear. When you catch yourself going there, take a moment to use the breathing exercise from before, connect with the present moment, focus on the outcome you want—and act on it.

Meditation

One of the most powerful tools to reduce stress is meditation. Done well, meditation helps you become calmer, less reactive, and more aware of your emotions. It also creates a pause between stimulus and action, allowing you to act from intention rather than impulse. This is tremendously helpful in your relationships, where buttons are often easily pushed and feelings quickly hurt.

So what kind of meditation should you do? Almost any type can confer benefits on the CEO. They generally fall into one of three categories: focus, visualization, and observation. **Focus** meditation involves practices like staring at a candle or paying attention to your breathing. Mindfulness and Zen are both forms of focus meditation. This type is often used by beginners because it gives the mind something to do and thus calms it. **Visualization** meditation involves imagining something, like going to a peaceful meadow or seeing colors and energy in your body. Yoga Nidra is a popular visualization that is done lying down. Meditation apps such as Insight Timer, Calm, Waking Up, and Headspace offer good solutions for both focus and visualization meditation. **Observation** meditation, which includes Transcendental Meditation and Vedic meditation, is in some ways the easiest and in other ways the hardest type. It's the easiest because it requires nothing other than sitting, mentally repeating a mantra, and observing the thoughts that go by in your mind like clouds crossing the sky. But it's also the hardest because of the perception that meditation doesn't work when your mind is busy. The opposite is true: In observation meditation, a busy mind during a session is a sign the meditation is actually working. It's not that the mind has become busy during meditation; it's that you are now aware of it.

If you're serious about meditation, Transcendental Meditation is worth looking into. It requires learning from an instructor, typically over a couple of hours a day for four days, and can have a pronounced effect on peace of mind, lasting even later in the day when you aren't meditating. When Transcendental Meditation came to the United States in the 1970s, hundreds of studies were conducted that showed the health benefits of regular meditation. Today, it's practiced by many high-performing athletes and business leaders. Ray Dalio, one of the most successful investors in the world and founder of Bridgewater Associates, posted the following on LinkedIn in August 2022: "I practice Transcendental Meditation and believe that it has enhanced my open-mindedness, higher-level experience, equanimity, and creativity. It helps slow things down so that I can act calmly even in the face of chaos . . . It has helped me and many other people and I recommend that you seriously consider exploring it."

Beginning a meditation practice can be as simple as setting a pleasant timer for two to five minutes first thing in the morning to focus on your breath. Notice the breath going in and out of your nose, in and out of your chest, in and out of your belly.

As you notice your mind getting distracted with thoughts and to-do lists, return back to the next inhale, the next exhale. Over time, you can increase the length of your meditation to fifteen or twenty minutes. Most people who do a thirty-day meditation challenge find themselves loving the benefits so much that they miss it when they don't meditate.

THREE QUICK MINDFULNESS TIPS

Mindfulness is a practice, and it's not something you will instantly achieve or never mess up. Sometimes you'll forget, and sometimes you won't live up to your expectations. That's okay, because it's not about being perfect. No one is harder on an achiever than they are on themselves, but give yourself grace when you do find yourself once again distracted, stressed, or prey to your emotions. Perfection is a fake standard, unattainable, and often an excuse for failure. Rather, make excellence the standard and accept when you fall short. You only control your actions and your attitude, nothing else.

Here are three final thoughts that may aid you on your path toward mindfulness:

Doubt Your Doubts

Some people are confident all the time, but most of us are not this way. As we've discussed, it's natural for the mind to create scenarios where things don't work out, resulting in anxiety, worry, and stress.

In addition to recentering in the present and focusing on the outcome you do want, one way to deal with doubt is to use the mind's energy against itself and *doubt your doubts*. When your mind wants to say "I'm so worried this bad thing will happen," counter it by saying, "Yeah right! It won't happen!" You'll often find that this diminishes the power of the negative thought in your mind.

Replace Expectation with Appreciation

We all have certain expectations of people in our lives, and as CEOs we certainly have high expectations of the people we work with. When people don't live up to those expectations, it can lead to judgment and disharmony.

To stay mindful when a disappointment like this happens, take a moment to first appreciate the person for what they are doing right, for who they are. When you focus on the positive, a flood of gratitude will follow, shifting the energy in the situation. As CEO, in some cases you will need to hold a person accountable for a commitment they did not fulfill. But in many other cases, this initial pause for appreciation and mindfulness may help you see that your expectation was unfounded or not understood—perhaps because the person operates with a very different personality from yours, as we discussed in Part I. Ultimately, allowing yourself to remain upset over unmet expectations only causes you harm. Choose appreciation instead, if only for your own happiness.

Practice the Art of Allowing

Each one of us is the main character of our own unfolding story. We each have our mission, our supporting cast, our good times and challenging times, and a thread that runs from the beginning of the story and ties in to its end.

The author of any good story guides their characters through the ebbs and flows of their journey. All that is left for these characters to do is to allow the story to unfold. To trust. And turn the page to see what happens next.

This is not unlike the story of your life. It will unfold, moving forward just like it has unfolded for years and years in the past. Despite the ups and downs, you are okay. You are reading this book. The ground has not vanished from beneath your feet.

Rather than stressing about the future, holding on to expectations of what it should look like, and generally—like many CEOs—being a control freak, try relaxing and *allowing* your life to unfold. You can't force a flower to unfold its petals, and you can't force something to happen in your life that is not ready to happen. Furthermore, resisting *what is* makes it more difficult for the current to flow, for new windows to open, for magic to happen. Instead of resisting this moment, allow this moment and every moment thereafter. Then watch what happens!

ACTION ITEMS: BUILD YOUR PLAYBOOK

- **Do the eulogy exercise.**

- **Establish your AM and PM bookends.**

- **Put weekly Deep Work and Deep Love blocks on your calendar.** Stick with these commitments.

- **Consider establishing a daily meditation practice.**

CONCLUSION

TIME TO IMPLEMENT

A system is only as good as its implementation. You now know all the parts of the Chief Executive Operating System, and we hand the baton off to you to begin applying it to your organization.

To help you along, we have collected the cornerstone exercises of the CEO-S playbook at **AmericanCEO.com / playbook**. Get these fundamental items in place first. From there, you can continue your journey toward becoming the best CEO possible—deepening your understanding of people, applying your time to each of the five responsibilities, mastering the skills of the CEO, and growing your mindfulness.

Applying the system *does* take discipline. Getting into an operating rhythm requires consistency. Thinking about the future can be hard. Dealing with people isn't always fun. Our hope, however, is that with a comprehensive system at your disposal, you will feel more empowered to do the things that need to be done, when they need to be done, so that you can deliver predictable performance.

Finally, should you find yourself needing support, we would be happy to connect you with a Chief of Staff who is trained in the Chief Executive Operating System. Having a competent, business-minded Chief of Staff / lieutenant / right-hand person at your side can make a world of difference. Email us at info@ AmericanCEO.com if you would like a referral.

We wish you great luck in this challenging but highly rewarding role. Stay in touch.

ACKNOWLEDGMENTS

Properly acknowledging the people who contributed to our understanding of effective CEO leadership would require too many pages to include here. Among these people are countless mentors, friends, colleagues, bosses, and family members spanning back to our earliest years.

However, we would like to particularly thank the leaders who have attended CEO training with American CEO over the past several years. Your enthusiasm for mastering the chief executive role, and your willingness to share your struggles and successes, has been inspiring. We have learned immensely from you.

We would also like to thank the team that helped us edit, design, and release this book. Barbara Schirmer and Aaron Hierholzer's sharp eyes helped shape and refine the text, while Sheila Parr lent her outstanding design talents to the book's interior and cover. This book also marks our third collaboration with Sam Scholl, now officially our favorite audiobook narrator. We enthusiastically thank Michael Beas and Dar Dowling for their ongoing work to promote this book and the message behind it. We would also like to acknowledge our mighty team at American CEO and the Trammell Group, including Ben Erwin, Noah Sakr, and Elana Hannah. Their efforts power the organizational mission—to build up and support world-class CEOs—of which this book is just one part.

ABOUT THE AUTHORS

Joel Trammell has spent more than thirty years serving as CEO of companies ranging from technology startups to a public company. He has twice founded and led startups to nine-figure exits. A leading CEO educator, Trammell regularly speaks at conferences and events nationwide. He has contributed to *Entrepreneur*, *Forbes* and Inc.com, and has served on the boards of public, private and nonprofit organizations. He is also the owner of *Texas CEO Magazine*, the founder of Texas CEO Ranch, and the previous author of *The CEO Tightrope* and *The Manager's Playbook* (with Alicia Thrasher).

Joel's latest endeavor is American CEO, through which he offers in-person training on the CEO role to small cohorts of world-class leaders. He currently lives in Austin with his wife and their three children. In his free time, you might find him on his tennis court.

Sherif Sakr is the cofounder of American CEO. He comes from a diverse international background and a career that spans success in five industries, including business ownership. He has spent the last decade teaching and coaching individuals and CEOs to drive results while maintaining a mindful perspective to reduce stress and optimize fulfillment. Sherif is now on a mission to train and equip CEOs with tools, strategies, and systems so that their companies and employees can thrive.

www.ingramcontent.com/pod-product-compliance
Lightning Source LLC
Chambersburg PA
CBHW030123240326
41458CB00121B/400